How to Worship as a Presbyterian

Dean W. Chapman

Geneva Press
Louisville, Kentucky

Book design by Sharon Adams
Cover design and illustration by Rohani Design

First edition
Published by Geneva Press
Louisville, Kentucky

This book is printed on acid-free paper that meets the American National Standards Institute Z39.48 standard.⊗

PRINTED IN THE UNITED STATES OF AMERICA

01 02 03 04 05 06 07 08 09 10 — 10 9 8 7 6 5 4 3 2 1

Library of Congress Cataloging-in-Publication Data

A catalog record for this book is available from the Library of Congress.

ISBN 0-664-50158-3

Contents

Chapter 1

Three Dimensions of Worship

Let us . . . offer to God an acceptable worship.
—Hebrews 12:28

*W*e Presbyterians worship. Week after week, we gather together to repeat the familiar hymns, prayers, and creeds. We listen to anthem, scripture, and sermon. We make our offering. Worship is a part of the rhythm of our lives. And yet for some of us it seems that a certain emptiness has begun to creep into our experience of worship. You may know folks who find springs of living water in the weekly services, but you may also know someone who has sat in a worship service, in the midst of the announcements, the prayers, the hymns, the sermon, the creed, and asked, "Is that all there is?"

On the one hand, worship is certainly important; it is the backbone of the Christian faith, and has been for nearly 2,000 years. Human beings have worshiped since before the dawn of recorded history. It is the conscious act of worship that distinguishes human beings from all other animals. Monkeys and parrots make tools; whales and bees have language. We human beings alone are *homo religiosus.*

On the other hand, worship at times can seem like eating cardboard crackers—tasteless and with no nutritional value whatsoever. At such times, we are driven to wonder what on earth has kept people worshiping on a regular basis for so long. What are we getting out of this? What value does God find in our worship activities?

Yet in spite of our questions, it is still true that normal, healthy, intelligent people worship. And there is a reason. In order to understand why we go through all the hoopla of worship, it helps to understand something about the nature of worship itself.

Worship is a very big subject, and this is a very little book. It is obvious, therefore, that this book will not be covering every aspect of worship, not even every aspect of *Christian* worship. To give us a handle on the subject, let me set forth three prominent dimensions of the word *worship*: (1) worship as a mode of being, (2) worship as ritual, and (3) worship as work.

Worship as a Mode of Being

When we call worship a *mode of being,* we are saying that worship is an experience that lies deeper than conscious thought and is virtually impossible to contain, or even describe, in words. It functions on the level of assumptions, intuition, life rhythms, raw existence. When you get down below the level of worship in a human being, you've gotten down below the level of being human.

To better understand the term *mode of being,* let us look for a moment at the way in which work—a job, a career, child-rearing—is a mode of being for much of Western culture. There are obvious reasons we need a job (to eat, for instance), but the value of having a job, a career, is far greater than simply its ability to provide food. There is a rightness about employment; a sense that work is the proper activity for human beings. Most of us believe that our work is valuable. It is important to us to feel that we are contributing members of society. We like to be thought of as hard-working people; to be unemployed is to be stigmatized.

In one social sense, we are—at *all* times—what we *do.* The first question we ask in casual conversation with a stranger, after we learn his or her name, is, "What do you do?"

It isn't as if we wake up every morning and have to remind ourselves consciously about all this; it's *the way we are.* We *breathe* work. Being immersed in a career seems so natural to us that we can't imagine being any other way, and if for some reason we cannot be immersed in a career we love—because of disability, or underemployment, or sometimes just retirement—we feel the absence acutely.

Of course, we are not always on the job. Sometimes we are occupied with other responsibilities. We volunteer, we go on vacation. Sometimes we're out with friends. We eat, sleep, have hobbies and pastimes, take care of the house and car. But as a mode of being, our calling penetrates all of these activities—not consciously (unless we bring our assignments home with us), but in terms of the values we develop, the way we interact with people we meet, the approaches we take to solving problems, the elements of new situations that seem to impress themselves on us, even the casual clothes we wear.

If, for instance, I am a medical professional, I tend to notice health signs about people I pass casually in the grocery store; I read the instructions on just about every box or bottle of anything; I wash my hands differently than most people do even when I'm on vacation. News items pertaining to health draw my special attention, and I view them in a different light than other people do.

Being a health professional is a mode of being, far more encompassing than a 9 to 5 workday, and far more penetrating than the skills needed to perform my tasks. In shorthand, I might say, "I am a nurse. That is who I am. Periodically (say, from 3 to 11 five days a week), I am *employed* as a nurse; but whether I'm at the hospital or not, I *am* a nurse. It is my nature, my training; it's in my blood, it's a mode of being for me."

Similarly, we might think of parenthood as a mode of being. When we have children, we are not always doing specifically parenting acts, but we are always parents, consciously or otherwise. When we are actually changing a diaper, helping with homework, or attending a Little League game, our parenthood might be a little more obvious to us and others than when we are stuck in traffic on the way to work or corresponding with the IRS over a discrepancy in our refund. But whether or not we are in the moment doing uniquely parental tasks, we remain a parent, and not just in name only. Parenthood is a mode of being.

In a similar vein, worship is a mode of being for humankind. Worship is first of all a completely natural way of being human. At some level, worship is the natural way of being for all of God's creation. Evelyn Underhill writes: "By worship we mean the adoring response of the creature to the total demand of God, and the utmost contribution to His glory which it is able to make."[1] Or in the words of the psalmist:

Praise the LORD from the earth, you sea monsters and all
deeps, fire and hail, snow and frost, stormy wind fulfilling
[God's] command! Mountains and all hills, fruit trees and all
cedars! Wild animals and all cattle, creeping things and flying
birds!

Kings of the earth and all peoples, princes and all rulers of
the earth! Young men and women alike, old and young
together! Let them praise the name of the LORD. (Ps.
148:7–13)

What is true for all human beings is of course true for Christians. To really believe in God—not just accepting the possibility
that there might be a divine organizer, but to love God, to have
faith in God—is a mode of being that is always true for us,
whether or not we are doing anything specifically "religious" in
the moment. Worship is the ongoing response to the reality of
God, the way parenting is the ongoing response to the reality
of a child. Even when we're not conscious of it, we can't get
away from it!

If worship is a mode of being, then every Christian may say,
"I am—always—a worshiper. That is who I am. Periodically I
am *occupied* with worship, as when I am in the midst of a worship service. But *occupied* with worship or not, I am a worshiper.
It's my nature and my training; it's in my blood. Worship is a
mode of being for me."

The Religious Presence of Mind

I am always a parent, but there are certainly times when my
awareness of this particular mode of being is heightened. Within
the specific acts of parenting—reading a story, listening atten-
tively to an account of a rough day, explaining how a credit card
works—I am aware of a whole number of things at once. Things
like these:

> I don't have an instruction book for this job;
> I have an important role to play in this person's life;
> I love this person very much;
> I am very blessed by God.

I may be always a career person, but there are certainly times when my awareness of this particular mode of being is likewise heightened. I may have a day, or maybe even just fifteen minutes, when I experience that heightened awareness, and many thoughts flash through my mind at once, things like these:

> This job is cool!
> I'm good at what I do;
> I'm learning whole new skills;
> I am very blessed by God.

The term I will use for the heightened awareness we occasionally experience as a result of the worship mode of being is *religious presence of mind.* The religious presence of mind is an altered state of consciousness, in which all track of time is lost. We take pleasure and comfort in the performance of worship rituals, the sights and sounds of the sanctuary, the company of the saints around us. We are working, performing acts of love, for the majestic Creator God, who knew us before we were born, who breathes life into us every moment, and who will gather us in at life's end. This heightened awareness, this religious presence of mind, is absolutely critical to worship, because it indicates that we have entered the sanctuary of our soul. It is in the sanctuary of our soul that we meet God and share the actual conscious, personal, intuitive experience of truly worshiping.

If there is a drug in religion, it is the religious presence of mind, which provides a rush much as endorphins do for the athlete. But the drug of the religious presence of mind is not, as Karl Marx supposed, an opiate, deadening one's senses to the world. On the contrary, the religious presence of mind is the source of our deepest faith and strongest conviction. The religious presence of mind is the only drug that induces self-giving love.

Though one might rightly regard the mode-of-being meaning of the word *worship* as the most important meaning that could be ascribed to the word, I have a narrower focus here. Any work whose topic is worship will unavoidably make continuing reference to worship as a mode of being, and this book is no exception. My goal is more modest, though, and I refer the reader to such masterpieces as *The Divine Flame* or Evelyn Underhill's

Worship for more in-depth exploration of that dimension of worship. As vital as the subject is, this book is not primarily about worship as a mode of being.

Worship as Ritual

We also use the word *worship* to describe the actual, ritualized event of gathering to serve God. A social scientist would identify the acts performed (for instance, the Lord's Prayer, scripture reading, hymn singing, Communion) as religious acts, and would describe what takes place as "worship." All of us know from personal experience, however, that the ritualized event that the social scientist calls worship need not have any correlation at all to the mode of being understanding of worship described above. It is entirely possible to spend an hour in a church on Sunday morning and never lose track of time, never find the joy in worship that opens the doors of our souls, and consequently have no sense of awe, connectedness, and love that constitute the religious presence of mind, which reveals the presence of God.

Yet worship as *ritual* is absolutely essential to the experience of worship as a mode of being, and for this reason it is commanded by God. A person's mode of being (for example: careerist, parent), while always present subconsciously, or as an undercurrent, is totally dependent upon the regular experiences of the *formal* performance of one's duties. You have to actually *perform the rituals* of nursing (taking blood pressure, keeping charts, and so forth) in order to think, feel, behave, react, and plan as a nurse. If you change professions, or stop working completely, inevitably your mode of being starts to shift.

The same is true of worship. If you never actually perform the rituals of worship, eventually you lose worship as a mode of being entirely. You can no longer find the way to the door of the soul, and as a result, never experience the religious presence of mind. You are never prepared to meet God. True love for God, the love God commands, the love that sustains those who love, is centered in the religious presence of mind. And few people experience the religious presence of mind regularly, apart from the formal tasks of worship, that is, the rituals.

So God commands the formal acts of worship. The commands to worship occur throughout the Bible, but for some reason, we seem to have interpreted them in a rather abstract sense, unrelated to any specific time, place, group, or setting. "Praise the Lord" has lost much of its original worship setting, its power as a *command,* and has become simply a religious exclamation. Many a person with "praise the Lord" on his or her lips would be startled to hear the people sitting nearby suddenly comply with this request. Even in worship, we may find comfort in ritually repeating a phrase like "Serve the LORD with gladness!" (Ps. 100:2 RSV), but the very act of repetition seems to have deadened our hearts. "Serve the Lord with gladness!" is a specific instruction, not an abstract expression. It is a command to worship.

According to Jesus, the commandment that is first of all is, "You shall love the Lord your God with all your heart, and with all your soul, and with all your mind, and with all your strength" (Mark 12:30). Why does Jesus command us to love God? Isn't it bizarre to be *ordered* to love someone? It would seem that we either love someone or we don't. Being *told* to love someone really has little effect on how we feel about the person.

But Jesus is not talking about how we *feel.* Jesus is talking about what we *do.* He is assuming that the question, "which commandment is the first of all?" (Mark 12:28) would never even be asked, except by someone who already *feels* love for God, even if that love is mixed in with fear, doubt, distrust, distance—all those things that so often contaminate human love.

If you didn't already feel some love for God—even if only a sense of longing—you wouldn't be reading this book. So the first commandment is not a command to *feel* the emotions of love; it is to *do* particular loving acts. Those loving acts toward God, those rituals, taken together, are termed *worship.* There is no guarantee that this second dimension of worship—a prescribed regimen of ritual—will lead to the first dimension of worship— the mode of being, which is the groundwork for the religious presence of mind. But the Holy Spirit has revealed the rituals of Sunday morning as expressions of love acceptable to God. Regardless of the quantity of our passion for God, there is a way to express our love, and that is through ritual. Ritual, then, is the expression of obedience to the commandment that is "first of all."

This truth has sunk out of sight in much of our worship: *Ritual is our first expression of love for God.* The commandment to love God has often and rightly been interpreted to apply to a host of different situations, from saving the earth which God is creating (and loving), to being honest in business dealings, to reaching out to those in need. But all those ways of loving God are slightly indirect, like mowing the lawn as an act of love for my wife, or washing behind my ears as an act of love for my mother, or trusting my son with the car as an act of love for my son. Once in a while, I need actually to say, "I love you" face to face. Once in a while, I have to take my wife out on a date; once in a while, I have to call my mother; once in a while, I have to give my son a hug.

Surely God appreciates all the indirect love being offered up by Christians around the world; but once in a while, say, one hour out of every 168, we need to proclaim our love directly to God. So Jesus commands us, in the commandment that is first of all, to worship. Worship, in the sense of performing ritual, is therefore our first act of obedience to God, our number-one expression of love.

As vital as the specifics of ritual are to the actual expression of love for God, even a mere cataloging of the various Presbyterian rituals, to say nothing of a discussion of them, would require a far grander undertaking than this little book. Ritual is an essential dimension of worship, a dimension that is perhaps best explored with your pastor, using such resources from our tradition as the Directory for Worship in the *Book of Order.* Though I will be making reference to ritual in the following pages, my intent is not to determine, or even describe, proper ritual. This book is not about worship as ritual.

Worship as Work

This book is about worship as work. When we speak of worship as a mode of being, we are naturally considering the *why* dimension of worship. Experiencing the presence of God is *why* we value worship so much; *why* we study and discipline ourselves to perform the acts of worship, to do the work of worship. Worship as a mode of being is an intuitive, intensely personal experience, completely dependent upon the action of the Holy Spirit.

When we speak of worship as a series of rituals, we are considering the *what* of worship. We are trying to answer the question, *What* visible activities actually constitute the behavior of worship? Worship as a series of rituals is a matter of doctrine and denomination. We pose such questions as, What actions constitute valid baptism? Shall there be kneeling for prayer? Is there to be an Assurance of Pardon during Lent? This dimension of worship is so corporate in nature that whole discussions can take place without mention of any particular individual experience.

Worship as *work,* however, which is the subject of this book, deals with the *how* of worship. *How* am I, a worshiper in the pew, to perform the tasks that comprise the rituals of worship, through which I hope to experience the religious presence of mind?

How do I do my job of worship? This book attempts to answer this question for the average Presbyterian worshiper, the person in the pew. Worship as a mode of being is the pearl of great price; worship as ritual is the prescribed act of love that prepares the way; worship as work is the nuts and bolts without which nothing else happens.

Let me say quickly that I do not intend to equate *work* with *tedium.* There is already sufficient tedium in our worship services. The work God sets out for us is actually enjoyable, even celebrative; but it is still work.

I like to garden. I like to prepare the soil, arrange and plant landscapes, care for flowers and vegetables, and ultimately, enjoy the harvest. My back sometimes gets sore from all the bending, and I usually work up a good sweat, but overall, gardening is a pleasant experience for me. No matter how you look at it, though, gardening is work. There are no arcades at the mall attracting teenagers to spend their money for a chance to mix soil amendments or pull weeds. Gardening is *work.* It's just that it's worth it to me. Worship, likewise, is worthwhile *work.*

Wouldn't it be unnerving to be in a hospital where the doctors and nurses were not aware that they were there to *work?* Where the people passing you in the hall, or strolling into your room, had name tags identifying them as health professionals, but had no apparent awareness of what they were supposed to be doing, or that they were employed to accomplish specific tasks, aimed at getting you back to full strength? Wouldn't it disturb you to realize that the building was full of people who were all expecting someone *else* (the hospital administrator, maybe) to provide all the patient care? What do you suppose would be the level of physical health in such a hospital? Yet something akin to this atmosphere exists in our own churches whenever the worshipers do not understand worship to be *working* for God.

It is common knowledge that membership in mainline churches is in decline, and has been for some time. We have cast about for ways to reverse that decline, and some of us have looked to commercial enterprises for direction. *Repentance* has become a very negative word; now we try to *attract* worshipers. "Come in and sit in our pews," we say. "We have something to offer." Unfortunately, what people in a consumeristic culture hear is, "Come in and get your money's worth—be entertained."

I question whether it can be put into words how misguided, counterproductive, and unspiritual such an approach is. It exactly turns the tables of worship. Instead of working for God, the "worshiper" (what does that word mean in such a setting?) waits to be entertained by God. Church, the last hope for communion with God, has become one more theme park attraction. The last hole in the secular sky is plugged. This tragedy has been accomplished by losing sight of the truth that worship is work.

Worship is not just *any* work, of course. It is the very specific work of waiting upon God. Work in general is forbidden on the Sabbath, a commandment that by all rights should be much more carefully observed in our churches and fellowships today. In fact, worship is the *only* regular work that is permitted on the Sabbath, both in the Old Testament (for example, Num. 28:9) and the New (Matt. 12:5). Jesus refutes the Pharisees by pointing out that "on the sabbath the priests in the temple break the sabbath and yet are guiltless" (Matt. 12:5), that is to say, they do their work (worship) without being judged to be in violation of the fourth commandment.

The reason the priests are guiltless on the Sabbath is that they are working *in the Temple.* Jesus goes on to say, "I tell you, something greater than the temple is here" (Matt. 12:6). As Christians, we know what Jesus is talking about; to be in Jesus' presence is to be in the throne room of God. So, too, today, it is the presence of Jesus in our sanctuaries that sanctifies our work and renders us guiltless. ("For where two or three are gathered in my name, I am there among them," Matt. 18:20.) As I hope to make clear in the following pages, we are priests working in the House of God on the Sabbath, precisely in keeping with our Judeo-Christian heritage, as interpreted by our Presbyterian tradition.

Work as a Priest

The idea of this book is rooted in the Reformation doctrine of the "priesthood of all believers." I will take up the background and basis for this doctrine a little more deeply in chapter 2. The bottom line for you as a faithful follower of Jesus Christ, however, a believer who is committed to working for God in worship, is this: you are a priest. As a priest, you experience worship as a mode of being; as a priest, you perform the rituals of worship; as a priest, you work in worship. Your office and your title in worship is *priest.*

Imagine yourself getting a job at a large office building. You have a desk, a chair, a computer terminal, maybe a potted plant. All day long you do nothing but sharpen pencils and rearrange the paper clips in your top drawer, because you don't know what you're supposed to be doing. How long could such a job keep your interest? How long would you sit idly in the chair before you began to look at the clock and long for quitting time? How much more involved and interested would you be if you had some clue as to what the company was doing, and specifically, what you could be doing to help the company?

The early Reformers were quite convinced that every believer was a priest. And who should be informed about worship, skilled in ritual, and regular in performance of religious duties, if not a priest? If the church, then, can be thought of as a company, then each one of us, as a priest, is responsible for its spiritual success.

The aim of this book is to help you get a grip on your job description, so you don't have to fidget through an hour of worship, wondering how such an experience could possibly be furthering the reign of God. Think of the following chapters as a training manual for worship.

Too Much Work as a Priest?

Those of us raised many years ago in a worshiping congregation may reasonably ask why there should be a need for something like a training manual for worship. Isn't worship so much a part of being human that it comes naturally? Haven't Christians been worshiping for nearly 2,000 years? Well, yes and yes. I certainly don't mean to imply that a person has to have a seminary education to worship. It would be a tragedy beyond words for worship to be perceived as a specialization.

But our culture is changing, and like a boat without a rudder, the church is drifting along in a consumeristic current, "tossed to and fro and blown about by every wind of doctrine . . ." (Eph. 4:14). We are bombarded with subconscious messages that life is really about the exchange of money; that our place in the world is as a consumer; and that all our relationships should be built on the model of buying and selling. Such an approach to *anything,* including worship, always boils down to one question, and one question only: What am I getting out of it? There is no thought of service, no thought of family connection and responsibility.

Whether or not you believe this is any way to relate to other human beings, it is no way to relate to God. The effect of this consumeristic drift is that, without really being aware of how we got here, many Presbyterian congregations, and many Presbyterians, find themselves in a place where worship no longer seems natural, purposeful, meaningful. I will not be attempting any deep analysis as to how this drift took place. I am only suggesting that we set aside consumerism, at least as it relates to God, and return to our roots with a little more focus, a little more awareness, and a little more discipline, and play our part in the universal drama of Creation we know as worship.

Even though I stress throughout this book the dimension of

worship that is work, and even though virtually every chapter lays out duties for you as a priest to perform, I encourage you not to be misled into believing that worship is sinking under the weight of a thousand tasks. Worship *is* work; Jesus *does* say, "Take my yoke upon you" (Matt. 11:29), but he goes on immediately to say, "my yoke is easy, and my burden is light" (11:30). What St. Augustine says about the sacraments applies in reality to all the duties that our tradition calls upon us to fulfill—"very few in number, very excellent in meaning, very easy to observe."[2] Indeed any duties outlined below that are not what John Calvin calls "true exercises of piety" should simply be cast aside. But we Presbyterians recognize the value of work, and God deserves our best.

Outline and Method of Study

This book consists of eight chapters. You've already made it through the first. The next chapter deals with the priesthood of all believers, a doctrine central to the Reformation that birthed Presbyterianism, and critical to preparing the way of the Lord in those churches that are today's heirs of that tradition. Chapter 3 deals with prayer, chapter 4 with music, and so on. Each chapter contains a brief essay that serves as a backdrop for the duties related to the chapter's topic. The essay is followed by a list of duties. At the end of each chapter are review questions that help refresh the material covered and discussion questions that allow Sunday School classes and other groups to think about what they have read.

This book is about the worship of the church—the whole church. No one person can worship as the whole church worships, and it will be difficult indeed for one person, reading in isolation from the church, to derive much lasting spiritual guidance from this book. Each of us is a part of the whole, connected to the larger body. To imagine that one person's experience of worship will turn a corner in the spiritual journey while others around them remain unaware is to imagine that a set of windshield wipers can turn a corner while the car to which it is attached proceeds straight ahead. What I am saying is this: Read and study this book as a part of some small group in the church.

Read it through once on your own, if you like, to assure yourself that it has some merit. But then study it, select what is valuable from it, and apply it, *with a group.* It's hard to make music to God with the sound of one hand clapping.

REVIEW QUESTIONS

1. What three prominent dimensions of the word *worship* are discussed in this chapter?
2. Which of these dimensions addresses the *why* question of worship? Which addresses the *what* question? Which addresses the *how* question?
3. What term is applied to the heightened awareness of worship as a *mode of being*?
4. What is the relationship between the *rituals* of worship and the commandment that is first of all? (Mark 12:28–30)
5. Why is ritual necessary if we are to experience worship as a mode of being?
6. What is the central question this book attempts to answer for the Presbyterian in the pew?
7. What is your office (title) as you work in worship?

DISCUSSION QUESTIONS

1. What human condition is for you a *mode of being*?
2. Have you ever experienced the religious presence of mind while listening to or performing music? Studying or creating art? Observing nature? When else?
3. Which moments and activities in worship seem to be most obviously the fulfillment of duty? Which seem to be the least?
4. In your worship experience, is there a correlation between the performance of duty and the awareness of God?
5. On a scale of one to seven, with one being "negligible" and seven being "complete," how would you rate your own knowledge of worship?

Chapter 2

The Priesthood of All Believers

You shall be for me a priestly kingdom and a holy nation.
—Exodus 19:6

When we look at worship, what we find striking is the difference between the passion of those who gave birth to Protestantism—the Reformers—and the air of polite ignorance that permeates so many of our Presbyterian services today. The Reformers restructured worship to place the work for God in the hands of the priests in the pew. Today, the work for God has slipped back into the hands of worship "leaders"—pastors, associate pastors, music directors—and out of the hands of those whom we still refer to as "worshipers." Hymns are now understood to be for those who enjoy music; prayer is a time for rest and daydreaming; the offering is just there to make sure the bills are paid.

What has happened to the worship of God? What has become of the Protestant doctrine of the priesthood of all believers?

Heritage of the Doctrine

The doctrine of the priesthood of all believers was a central element in the Protestant Reformation. The great sociologist of religion Ernst Troeltsch once defined *Protestantism* as "a modification of Catholicism, in which the Catholic formulation of problems was retained, while a different answer was given to them."[1] One of the key questions to which Protestantism gave a radically different answer than that of Catholicism was, What is the church?

The Catholic answer was, "The church is the body of those ordained priests who minister to the laity through the performance of the mass." It was the "heresy" of Martin Luther, whose ninety-five theses triggered the Protestant Reformation, to claim that the true church is *the whole community* of Christian believers. The concept of the priesthood of all believers was one of the principles that earned Luther the designation of the antichrist, the "wild boar" that was ravaging God's vineyards, as the pope described the situation in the papal bull that excommunicated Luther from the Catholic Church in 1521.[2]

To the Protestant mind, however, the idea did not originate with Luther. Luther himself points to the Bible, to scripture, as the source of his belief:

> We are all consecrated priests through baptism, as St. Peter says in 1 Peter 2 [verse 9], "You are a royal priesthood and a priestly realm."[3]

Luther was not alone in this conviction. John Calvin, founder of the Reformed branch of Protestantism, from which we Presbyterians have sprung, wrote in his *Institutes of the Christian Religion* that "in [Christ] we are all priests . . . to offer praises and thanksgiving, in short, to offer ourselves and ours to God."[4]

In the seventeenth century, John Smyth and other early Baptists made much of this Protestant concept, bequeathing it to later Baptists.[5] W. B. Shurden, Baptist scholar and author of an entire book entitled *The Doctrine of the Priesthood of Believers,* writes that this doctrine is "the centerpiece of the Baptist faith."[6]

There can be no doubt, then, that the leaders of the faith that launched Protestantism were firmly convinced that all believers are priests; and further, that this article of faith was, and is, rooted in scripture (1 Peter 2:5, 9; Rev. 1:5–6; 5:9–10; 20:6), which for Protestants "holdeth forth a most perfect rule, wherunto nothing may be added, nor from it may aught be diminished."[7]

Connotations of the Word *Priest*

In order for the doctrine of the priesthood of all believers to make a difference in our day-to-day lives as Christians, of course, the word *priest* must have some practical application; it must stand for something. While a dictionary might leave the impression that it is a simple matter to define the word *priest,* within the realm of religion, the word has a number of slightly different meanings. *Priest* denotes certain specific persons in various traditions, and the word also carries a whole host of connotations— of spirituality, dress, role in society, and so forth.

In fact, if we try to make any claims for the meaning of the word *priest,* we must fight through an army of preconceived notions, everything from long-stored memories of watching an aborigine ritually kill a goat on a *National Geographic* special, to listening to a man in a clerical collar make an appeal for disaster aid on the local news. Maybe we visited a cathedral once and saw men moving silently in long robes; or maybe we have read Graham Greene's *The Power and the Glory,* about a priest in rural South America who finds meaning in his own faith. Putting aside all these images to reexamine the meaning of the word *priest* is no easy undertaking.

The stumbling block to thinking of ourselves as priests lies not in our heritage or in our understanding of our duties, but in all these connotations that have accrued to the word *priest* up to the age in which we live. The problem began with the Reformation itself. To distance ourselves from the Roman Catholic Church, we deliberately steered clear of referring to ourselves as priests, even though, as noted, the founders of the major Protestant movements have embraced the doctrine of the priesthood of all believers. We let the word *priest* drift away from us, and now it seems out of place in our churches. Our religious identity has been shaped in part by the *absence* of "priest" in our vocabulary of faith.

The understandable consequence of this development has been that, with no developed Presbyterian sense of the word, *priest* has been shaped ever more closely over the centuries of Western culture to the Roman Catholic tradition. To think of myself as a priest in America today carries with it the connotation that I am thinking of myself as a Roman Catholic.

One of the dimensions of the Catholic understanding of *priest* is the strong boundary that exists between the priesthood and the laity (the people in the pew). Since the Catholic idea of *priest* is by far the dominant one, it is only natural for us to suppose that a person has to be somehow different to be a priest—religiously dressed, celibate, financially supported by the church. Since it is hard to attach any of these characteristics to the average Protestant, the word *priest* no longer seems to fit us.

Matters have grown worse in the highly technological society in which we live, a society that has stressed specialization in every professional field. From law advice to love advice, from internal medicine to interpersonal relationships, every branch of inquiry, every group of society, has its experts, its specialists. It is only natural, then, to look for specialists in the church. The term *priest* is a handy tool for labeling such specialists, and every time it is applied, the wedge is driven deeper between those who lead worship and those in the pews.

There is no easy way to set aside these cultural conceptions. Today the rift seems to be widening between those who "conduct" worship and "ordinary" Christians. The tragedy is that this rift destroys the Presbyterian understanding of worship, and deprives most of us of what we hunger for—the religious presence of mind. This widening rift is a principal reason why so many raised in the Presbyterian tradition have given up attending church. They can no longer see the point of worship! We have let the doctrine of the priesthood of all believers slip through our fingers; we have lost our grip on the fundamental truth that *it is precisely through the fulfillment of our priestly duties*—not through intellectual analysis, not through emotional mountaintop experiences, not through attaching ourselves to some charismatic preacher—*that we come to learn how to "walk humbly with our God."* The path to God is in our *genes* and in our *routines.*

There is, I suppose, one "up" side to the fact that for about 475 years, the term *priest* has not generally been applied to anyone of the Presbyterian faith. There *are* no hidden connotations about Presbyterian priests. The slate is clean. So setting aside as best we can the connotations we have of priests from other religious traditions, let us approach afresh the doctrine of the priesthood of all believers by looking again at the fundamental meaning of the word *priest.* Let us begin by asking the question, How did we get to be priests in the first place?

A Priest by Inheritance

How does one become a priest? How are people set apart for special religious duties? Do we become priests by performing tasks in church, like praying for each other, singing the Doxology, or reading scripture? In attempting to answer these questions, the Presbyterian's first and natural response is to turn to scripture.

Jewish law (our Old Testament) decreed that only one family—the descendants of Levi—could be priests. (There came to be a narrowing of the priesthood even within the tribe of Levi: When *priest* and *Levite* occur together, the former is a descendant of Aaron [himself *one* line of Levitical descent], and the latter is descended from another branch of Levi's family; these "Levites" served as assistants to the priests.)

It fell to members of the Levite family to conduct God's business in the Temple. They made known God's will, ritually slaughtered animals, conducted worship, cared for the sanctuary, pronounced the blessing, and so forth. *Only* the descendants of Levi could perform these priestly functions. No one else, no matter how devout his faith, was permitted to serve as a priest.

In fact, the writer of Hebrews argues that Jesus is a priest "after the order of Melchizedek" (7:17 RSV) because Jesus lacked the *genealogy* to be a Jewish priest. He was not a member of the tribe of Levi. "For the one of whom these things are spoken belonged to another tribe, from which no one has ever served at the altar. For it is evident that our Lord was descended from [the tribe of] Judah" (Heb. 7:13–14 RSV).

This limitation of the priesthood to the family of Levi had three important ramifications. First, the priesthood was not something you could aspire to; you had to belong to the family. It was your lineage, not your intelligence, commitment, piety, wealth, education, personality, or any other characteristic that opened the door to the priesthood. Only one question need be answered: Who are your parents?

Second, if you were a member of the family, you were *automatically* on track to become a priest. You did not apply for the position—it was simply expected of you. From your youth, you were instructed in the duties of the Temple, as naturally as we learn our multiplication tables today. Parents were proud to follow the stages of training, but no one oohed and aahed over it; it was the natural course of events.

And third, since there were many sons of Levi, but only one Temple, there were far more priests than there was money to support them. This meant that the average priest held down a full-time job (usually as a farmer) and rotated into the service of the Temple according to a schedule. Zechariah, for instance, the father of John the Baptist, was serving his appointed time as priest in the Jerusalem Temple when the angel appeared to him (Luke 1:8–11), even though his home was in the hill country (1:39).

These three ramifications shape the Christian priesthood as well, but only the third, the volunteer nature of the priesthood, is perhaps immediately obvious. You are a *volunteer* priest. You serve God on Sunday mornings, but your livelihood comes from a source other than the church. Of the second ramification—the naturalness of the training—we have to admit that our tradition has left much to be desired. My hope is that this book will contribute in some way to rectifying this lack. For the moment, however, let us look at the first ramification—namely, that your lineage, the family to which you belong, is the sole determining factor in whether or not you are a priest.

Our Own Adoption

According to Hebrews, a new priesthood was established with Jesus, "after the order of Melchizedek." Who belongs to this new priesthood? If *lineage* is the determining factor, and it is Jesus who has established the priesthood, the priesthood should consist of all who belong to Jesus' family.

John writes: "To all who received him, who believed in his name, he gave power to become children of God" (John 1:12). As Paul informs the church at Ephesus, "So then you are no longer strangers and aliens, but you are citizens with the saints and also members of the household of God" (Eph. 2:19) and later, "Gentiles have become fellow heirs" (3:6). The truth is set out boldly in 1 John 5:1: "Everyone who believes that Jesus is the Christ has been born of God." Thus to restate the familiar line "Jesus is our

brother," to declare that we are children of God, is also to identify ourselves as members of the *priestly* family.

The ultimate source of this belief is Jesus himself. In the
Mediterranean world of the first century of the common era, family ties were what held society together. For better or worse, a
person was woven far more tightly into the fabric of the family
than we are in the United States today. We do not feel the shock,
then, that Jesus' neighbors must have felt when Jesus, summoned
by his mother and brothers, created a whole new family for himself. "And looking at those who sat around him, he said, "Here
are my mother and my brothers! Whoever does the will of God is
my brother and sister and mother" (Mark 3:34–35).

Those same words live in our sanctuary when we worship.
Jesus looks around at us gathered together and declares us to be
his sisters and brothers. Jesus himself has adopted us into the
priestly order, his priestly family.

So by adoption into the family of God, we have been granted
the honored lineage and the special responsibilities associated with
the worship of God. We have become priests. Thus our priesthood
is a gift from God, an honor we inherit as God's children.

So What Does a Priest *Do*?

Since the "great high priest" of Hebrews 4:14 is our *brother,* we
are all priests. What does it mean, in practical day-to-day terms,
to be a member of a priestly family? How are we any different as
priests than we would be if we weren't priests?

The Priest as Sacrificer

One way to define the word *priest* is functional. What does a
priest *do*? If it can be shown that a priest's function is in some
way unique, then the term has meaning, and anyone who is regularly authorized and assigned to those functions, anyone who is
expected to and does in fact fulfill those functions, is properly
termed a *priest.*

Perhaps the one word most frequently associated with *priest* is
the word *sacrifice. Sacrifice* comes from the Latin words mean-

ing *sacred* and *make,* or *do.* In its broadest religious sense, it means *to do something sacred,* to perform an act for God. If we take *sacrifice* in its broadest sense, we must understand the priest to be one who sacrifices, one who does sacred things in a holy place (temple, church, shrine).

The word *sacrifice* has also acquired a narrower religious meaning, namely that of ritual killing. It can hardly be denied that one function of priests throughout the millennia of human existence has been the performance of sacrificial slaughter. The lamb of the Passover meal, for instance, had to be sacrificed by a priest in the Jerusalem Temple. In one sense, sacrificial slaughter was one of the chief businesses of the Temple, and the priests were the people who carried on this business.

It would of course be impossible to claim that you, as a Presbyterian in America today, are a priest, if being a priest by definition entails the ritual slaughter of animals. Such rituals have never been a part of Christianity as we know it. That the word does not *necessarily* entail such duties is clear from all the Reformers mentioned above, whose congregations most certainly did not engage in the religious sacrifice of animals in any way, shape, or form. Yet the Reformers regarded their congregations as a priesthood.

In all probability, the function of ritual slaughter was not essential to the understanding of the word *priest* in the New Testament. Most likely the congregations to which 1 Peter and Revelation are addressed did not participate in animal sacrifice either (see 1 Peter 2:9–10; Rev. 1:5). Thus the biblical writers, and later, the Reformers, were of one mind in considering the duties of priesthood to be defined in terms other than those of the slaughter of animals.

As Presbyterians, we believe that the whole idea of sacrifice underwent a change when Jesus died on the cross. Previously, sacrifice had been for the purposes of atonement and propitiation. In other words, the worshipers believed that God was angry with them because of their sins; by offering the blood of animals (instead of their own!), they believed they could cancel out (that is, *atone for*) their sins, and win back the good will of (that is, *propitiate*) God. Jesus, however, was the *perfect* sacrifice of atonement and propitiation, a lamb without blemish or spot. In offering himself on the cross, he performed these functions of sacrifice for the last time. "[Jesus] has no need, like those high priests, to offer sacrifices daily, first for his own sins and then for those of the people; he did this once for all when he offered up himself" (Heb. 7:27 RSV).

On the other hand, the New Testament still mandates sacrifice: "Through [Jesus] then let us continually offer up a sacrifice of praise to God, that is, the fruit of lips that acknowledge his name" (Heb. 13:15 RSV; see also Eph. 5:2 RSV), or again, ". . . present your bodies as a living sacrifice, holy and acceptable to God, which is your spiritual worship" (Rom. 12:1 RSV). The requirement for sacrifice is completely in keeping with the assertion that we are all priests. But if Jesus completed the work of atonement and propitiation once for all, then the word *sacrifice* must be freed from association with ritual slaughter, and must be thought of in its broader sense as "*whatever* work the priest does as a service to God."

The question then becomes, which acts *now* constitute sacrifice, the priestly duties we are to accomplish in the times and places set apart to God? What does Paul mean when he writes, "present your bodies as a living sacrifice"? To answer this question, it will help to look further at the traditional roles of priests in religion.

Ancient Duties of Priests

From before the beginning of recorded history, almost every culture has set apart certain persons for religious purposes—priestly duties—among which are: (1) taking care of holy places and holy objects, (2) performing religious rituals, and (3) communicating with the Divine. Often other duties have been assigned, other authority granted. According to Julius Caesar, for instance, the Druids (priests of the Celtic tribes of Britain, Ireland, and France) helped elect kings, served as ambassadors, studied astronomy, and executed criminals. Nearly every priesthood, however, has been charged with the three broad categories of duties enumerated above. They bear repeating:

1. The care of holy places and holy objects
2. The performance of religious ritual
3. Communication with the Divine

In this regard, Christianity has much in common with other religions. Almost anyone from a Christian background, even if he or she has only a vague sense of the meaning of the word *priest,* will find something to relate to in this list of functions. The careful handling of the paraments (the religious cloths that adorn the front of many sanctuaries, for example, the Bible bookmark, the Communion table cloth) might be an example of the care of holy places and objects; a chant accompanying the burning of incense might come to mind in imagining the performance of religious ritual; someone kneeling in a monk's cowl at an altar to pray might serve as an image of communication with the Divine.

In our own Sunday morning worship of God, we see that these three functions must still be maintained; and in point of fact, we perform them ourselves, behaving like priests even if we're not aware of doing so. If you help straighten up the sanctuary after worship, wash Communion cups, or mow the church lawn, you are performing the priestly function of caring for religious places and objects. When you say the Lord's Prayer in worship, participate in a responsive reading, or sing the Doxology, you are performing the priestly function of religious ritual; and of course, when you pray for loved ones, or listen to the scripture reading and sermon, you are communicating with God.

Priests Do "House" Work

Granted that we have been adopted by God, that we are properly and truly called "children of God," and so have become priests, we may assume that our duties include those traditionally associated with priests, namely: (1) the care of holy places and objects, (2) the performance of religious ritual, and (3) communication with God. What does all that mean in terms of day-to-day living?

In Jesus' culture, it was no small matter to be adopted into a family. To be adopted as a child, rather than remain a slave, meant that you now belonged not merely economically, but by blood. You were now a part of family discussions and decisions; you had a place at the family table; you related to your community as a member of a family, rather than as a servant. What being adopted did *not* mean was that now you didn't have to work.

In our day of wealth, we may imagine that in becoming sons and daughters of God, rather than servants, we have completely switched roles and functions within the reign of God, much as Cinderella did as she went from servant girl to princess. But in Jesus' day, the change in position didn't bring such a world of difference in its wake. That is to say, the day after your adoption as a daughter or son, you would most likely find yourself working right along with the servants, just as you had the day before, to make a go of the family farm.

Take a look at the parable of the prodigal son, for example (Luke 15:11–32). Odds are, the day after the celebration, both sons were out in the field working. Matthew also reports Jesus' story of a man sending his two sons to work in the vineyard (Matt. 21:28–32). Jesus does not mince words in explaining to his followers that we are expected to work (Luke 17:7–10). As far as the daily routine of work was concerned, it was all pretty much the same for children and servants alike.

And the "work" required of the first priestly family, that of Levi, was first of all "House" work, that is, work in the House of God (the Temple). To be a member of the priestly family was not simply some abstractly religious affair—it was a very tangible thing for the people of Jesus' day. It is reasonable to assume that being a priest affected the level of affection felt toward other priests, and it probably affected the general level of morality they exhibited in their daily lives. But to be a member of God's priestly family had some very practical, specific consequences as well. These consequences all revolved around the Temple.

To all the Jews of the first century, including Jesus, his disciples, the crowds that followed him, the Pharisees who opposed him, and the many who were hardly even aware of him, God had a particular home on earth. God's "street address" was the Temple, Jerusalem, Judea.

That particular building, with its courts, its sacrifices, its music and ritual, its customs and festivals, was the *home* of God. And like any home, it had its meals (burnt offerings), its family traditions, its celebrations, and of course its daily routines and physical maintenance—wood to be gathered for the fires, bread to be baked, cleaning, polishing, repairs. *All* of these duties fell to the priests. They "ran" God's house, doing anything and everything that was necessary for its operation.

The House Changes Hands

This very same Temple was the chief piece of property Jesus inherited as God's son. What could be more natural, especially in that time and place, than for the son to inherit the house and grounds that belonged to his family? In fact, this whole business of inheriting God's house was precisely what triggered Jesus' arrest, trial, and death. Inheritance was at the center of economic and social life, and if you claimed as your inheritance a house already occupied by others, bloodshed was likely.

If we follow Mark's account of the last week of Jesus' life, we see that what precipitates the conflict between Jesus and the Sanhedrin is the so-called cleansing of the Temple (Mark 11:15–19). By his actions, Jesus was making a claim to have inherited God's House (as God's son, naturally), and the House was now his responsibility. But the Levitical priests believed that *they* were responsible for the House of God. *They* were the ones who took care of the Temple precincts and functions on God's behalf. When Jesus attempted to discharge his responsibilities by driving out the money changers and prohibiting commercial traffic through the Temple court, they challenged his claim to having inherited the House of God: "By what authority are you doing these things? Who gave you this authority to do them?" (Mark 11:28).

From such a great distance, we easily lose sight of how important the House of God was to both Jesus and the Sanhedrin. While it is true that, in the same week that Jesus "cleansed" the Temple, he predicted that it would be destroyed, it nevertheless remained true also, in the eyes of first-century Jews, including Jesus and the disciples, that the Temple property was *God's,* and that a new Temple would be built on the same spot. We have no special need for the Temple in Jerusalem, but Jesus did—that's why he cleansed it. And so did the Sanhedrin. Even Jesus' accusers were sure that he was planning to put up a new Temple if he destroyed the old one (see Mark 14:58; 15:29).

The existing Temple had to be destroyed because the "tenants" in Jesus' parable (Mark 12:1–10; *not* the *children* of the owner) had killed the son; but the *property* on which the Temple stood would of course endure. God's plan was to give it to "others" (Mark 12:9). The "others" in the parable were most likely understood to be the faithful, namely Jesus' followers, the group that would in reality become the church. The "others," that is, the church, and ultimately, you and I, would then have exactly the same responsibilities toward the new Temple as the Levitical priests had had toward the earlier one.

Note that these "others" do not *buy* the vineyard, or *earn* it, or take it by force. They receive it from the owner as a *gift*. In those days, when an owner *gave* his real property to others, the act created a relationship tantamount to adoption. Real property was invariably passed on to one's children. Very seldom was it sold, because it represented the whole family's wealth. In those days, even more than in these, a person's real property was his or her riches, security, life's achievement, and even to a certain extent, *identity*. To bestow one's estate on others was to adopt them as one's children, in the eyes of both giver and recipients. Everyone who witnessed such a transaction would understand it in such a light. Thus the "others" whom God had chosen to be the new caretakers of God's property (that is, the Temple's new priests) would be treated not as strangers or even servants, but as children of the owner. They would *inherit* the House of God.

It would then fall to those adopted children to take care of the owner's (God's) property, to fulfill all priestly responsibilities. As the Temple was transferred from the first priestly family to the last, "child of God" and "priest" were merged into one. Whoever believed in Jesus was a child of God and therefore had priestly responsibilities in the (coming) House of God. To deny someone priestly responsibilities was to deny them membership in the family of God.

And leaping ahead some 2,000 years, this is precisely where we find ourselves today. God's house has diversified, one might say, into many buildings spread around the world. One of those buildings is occupied by your congregation. As a child of God, a member of the priestly family, it is your responsibility to perform whatever tasks are necessary to keep the House of God in order and functioning properly. Worship is of course the main function, but you have inherited the property, too. You have a responsibility for the heating and air-conditioning, the carpet, the restrooms, the pew racks, the choir robes, the lawn. You received this commission the moment you were adopted into the household of God. The House of God is now yours; so is the "House" work.

"House" Work and the Religious Presence of Mind

If we were to pinpoint the single most distinguishing characteristic of priestly experience, that characteristic which is hardly to be found anywhere else, and yet is desired above all others, it would be what I referred to in the last chapter as the religious presence of mind. It is the heightened awareness of our worship mode of being; the keen sense that we are working for God, in God's presence, giving glory to God, and sharing in the glory of God. It is the realization that we are surrounded by saints and angels, a great cloud of witnesses, the heavenly host. It is a sense of belonging, of being eternally *home*; a sense of rightness, of deep spiritual contentment. It is the experience of faith, the whole of which fills the soul to overflowing with joy, peace, grace, mercy, love.

The source and fountainhead of the religious presence of mind is the *work* we do as priests in worship. This source and fountainhead has dried up as we have lost sight of our priestly identity and duties. In those duties, responsibilities, tasks, lies the Way we seek. The magic, however, is not in the tasks themselves. Any work, even the most mundane, can be sacred; any work, even in the church, can be secular. Where or when such work takes place has little bearing on its sacredness.

As I mentioned earlier, we become priests through the act of adoption. *God* makes us priests. We worship because we are priests; we don't become priests by worshiping. Going a step further, we may say that it is not the work that makes the priest holy, but exactly the opposite: It is the priest who makes the work holy. *You* sanctify the hymnbook (and your lawn mower, computer, car, toothbrush, pen) by seeing it through the eyes of a priest, by permeating your use of it with your love of God.

In our technological, mechanistic age, in which the inert products of human production occupy vastly more space and material than we human beings do, and in which far more time is devoted to the production of substances than to expressions of substance, the prevalent model for understanding church work is now derived from manufacturing, a technology built upon the development of interchangeable parts. Unfortunately, it is *ourselves,* we human beings, who have become the interchangeable parts. Unconsciously we sense that, in a church as in a factory, there are necessary functions to be performed for smooth, efficient operation. These functions must be done by someone, some cog in the machine, but one person is as good as another, as long as he or she shows up on time and doesn't screw up. The *important* thing is that the task be accomplished. Someone must usher; someone must sing; someone must lead some kind of prayer; ultimately, some warm bodies must fill the pews.

What a bizarre way to regard worship! Worship is first of all spiritual—it is *critically* important who does the work. Worship is your act of love for God. No one can do it for you. You personally must be present, both physically and spiritually, for worship to matter at all. God isn't looking for numbers. God is looking for *you.*

There is no objective product of worship, some thingamabob that can be packaged, shipped, and sold. From a "production" point of view, worship is completely pointless and frivolous—as pointless and frivolous as giving your wife flowers, playing peekaboo with a one-year-old, or traveling across town to have Sunday dinner with your parents. Strange, isn't it, that God has created each of us specifically for such pointless and frivolous activities?

If we were automatons, we wouldn't need to worship at all. But we are spiritual beings—we hunger for God, we thirst for the religious presence of mind. And for this critical reason, our priestly duties of worship are not pointless or frivolous at all; they are the path of a meaningful, purposeful life. Through the fulfillment of our duties, we develop and strengthen a view of the world—God's view—which is denied to unbelievers.

The Eyes of Faith

You've probably seen a picture of what is called a "vase-face" illusion. It may appear to the viewer to be two faces looking at each other; or it may appear to be simply a vase. With a little practice, you can move back and forth from one perception to the other. One minute you see two faces, the next minute you see a vase. What has changed about the lines of the drawing? Absolutely nothing. We *see* something entirely different, but the actual lines are the same. We can speak of the two perceptions as parallel in that they exist "side by side," so to speak, but they never overlap. Seeing the vase means you can't see the faces; when you recognize the faces, you've completely lost sight of the vase.

There are parallel perceptions of the whole created universe, too. When you look at the world, you may see a living, beautiful world created by a loving, ever-present God, with a glory and a grandeur that the human mind can scarcely take in; or you may see an inert, mechanical lump of rock, whirling with no particular purpose, to no particular destination, in a cold, silent universe. The information our eyes provide us can be understood equally in either of these two parallel ways.

Jesus teaches us to see the world as the creation of a loving, ever-present God. And he does so not only through thought, as we attempt to understand his commandments, but also through routine, as his Spirit guides us in worship. Every single priestly duty contributes to our education. The hymns, the prayers (verbal and nonverbal), and the attentive listening open the inward eye to God, the Truth of Creation. For this reason, human beings have maintained the routine of worship for millennia.

This routine of worship is even more important in today's culture. We live in a secular society. We are bombarded daily with a secular view of the world; indeed we are immersed in it. As a result, we tend to think of the kingdom of God as something in the future. Blinded by our culture, we do not see the whole world as holy, shimmering with the presence of God. It *is* holy, and somewhere in our minds and souls, we *know* this, but when we look at the world, we don't *see* it. We see something ordinary, secular. Even worse, in that picture of creation as somehow ordinary or secular, we include ourselves.

When the day dawns that we see the world as we know it really is, when we experience everything as holy, from lawn mowers to lunar modules, from fungus to French fries, then we won't need to discipline ourselves to develop good worship habits. We won't hunger for a religious presence of mind, as something strange and elusive, because there won't be any *other* presence of mind, as there wasn't for Jesus. God will finally have answered our prayer that "Thy kingdom come, Thy will be done on earth."

This line from the prayer Jesus taught us is important to priests, because it indicates that God's kingdom is coming *to this earth*. What will be changing is not our location, but our *selves*. Being a priest means experiencing this change, flipping over, if you will, from the secular to the sacred, at least in worship. Our culture may teach us to interpret creation as lifeless, mechanical, material; but Jesus, through faith, opens our eyes to the truth— "The kingdom of God is at hand!" However, for the priest in the world, in whom cultural and Christian views of the world exist side by side, there exists the danger that, without even thinking about it, we can slide from one to the other.

I cannot stress this strongly enough: The "jobs" given to priests, which I will be discussing in the remainder of this book, are not simply things that must be done by somebody or other, as if worship were a product that churches manufacture. Priestly duties serve two functions. They (a) express our love for God, as we obey the commandment which is first of all: "You shall love the Lord your God with all your heart, and with all your soul, and with all your mind, and with all your strength"; and they (b) incorporate faith in us, strengthening the religious presence of mind. Should it come as any surprise that the God who creates and loves us commands us to do those very things that deepen our relationship with our Creator?

The path to God lies not primarily in penetrating, analytical thought, but in our genes and our routines, specifically our religious duties. To perform such duties without recognizing this primary and ultimate purpose is to be priests without being aware of what we're doing, to fall out of the kingdom of God and back into the secular world, even while we're right in the middle of a worship service! "Do not be conformed to this [the secular] world, but be transformed by the renewing of your minds" (Rom. 12:2).

Getting Down to Specifics

My aim in this chapter has been to demonstrate that the word *priest* within the Presbyterian tradition applies to *every* believer. To deny the priestly function is to deny a person membership in the family of God, to snatch away the opportunity to experience the religious presence of mind on anything like a regular basis.

Immersed in a sea of connotations associated with the word *priest,* we find it hard to reclaim the doctrine of the priesthood of all believers. Yet by inheritance in the family of God, through our own theological roots and traditions as Presbyterians, and in our own customs and habits of Sunday morning worship, we are naturally priests. Our souls require the education that the priesthood entails, and to ignore our priestly duties is to set ourselves up for spiritual starvation.

If I have been successful in making the claim of our priesthood, I have only set the stage for the question that will occupy the rest of this book, namely, What are our priestly duties in the Sunday morning worship hour?

REVIEW QUESTIONS

1. What was Martin Luther's "heresy" regarding the nature of the church?
2. What is the stumbling block to thinking of ourselves as priests?
3. How do we come to learn how to "walk humbly with our God"?
4. How did we become priests?
5. What three categories of duties do we have in common with *all* priests?
6. Which house is referred to in the expression, "a priest's 'housework' "?
7. What two purposes are accomplished by the performance of priestly duties?

DISCUSSION QUESTIONS

1. What is your image of priests? What makes them different from you?
2. Which elements, or times, in your worship service create in you the strongest sense of serving God, doing something that God finds pleasant?
3. What do you think of as a Christian's responsibilities in worship?
4. Can you recall a time in your life when you have experienced the religious presence of mind?
5. What would be the ideal relationship for you, between worship and the rest of your life?

Chapter 3

The Duties of the Priest: Prayer

Pray without ceasing.

—1 Thessalonians 5:17

Chapter 1 was devoted to the idea of worship as work. Weekly worship has specific times and places, specific tasks to be performed, specific functions to be fulfilled in the life of the individual believer, the corporate church, and the reign of God. Worship is many things, and one of the things worship is, is work.

Chapter 2 set forth the Protestant doctrine of the priesthood of all believers, the notion that the work of worship is the responsibility of everyone who believes and accepts Jesus Christ as Lord and Savior. Thus we might say that worship is our employment, and we are employees in the reign of God. To my way of thinking, worship is the best job in the world—our Employer is great and greatly to be praised (Psalm 48:1), the hours are good, the atmosphere on the job is refreshing, the results are truly meaningful, and the benefits are spectacular.

All that notwithstanding, however, worship is work, and to do it properly, we workers must follow some kind of job description. This and the following chapters will take up the specific duties and tasks that comprise Presbyterian worship.

The Most Important Duty

We begin with the first and most important duty of every priest in worship—prayer. Music is very important; preaching is very important; the offering is very important. But if one duty heads the list, it is the duty of prayer. Unfortunately, it is also becoming one of the most difficult tasks of the worshiper, because of the shallowing of America, the decreasing spiritual depth of our culture. All things truly religious are being swept away in a flood of consumerism. In a world where human beings are reduced to consuming objects, where image is everything and wisdom is a stranger, prayer dries up. It disappears from all but overtly "religious" activities, and even in worship services prayer sometimes seems no more than a hollow fossil of a once-living faith.

The knowledge of prayer, the images of devout people praying, even the very idea of prayer, is fading from the American consciousness like the memory of our grandparents after they've died. As the years pass, and fresh images are hammered into our consciousness, we still recognize the word *prayer*; we still believe we could define it. But many of us are uncertain, really, about what it's like to experience prayer.

The reason is not hard to find. America's consciousness is being shaped today by TV, with lesser contributions from the other media. Think of the TV shows you like to watch. Can you name a character from any of them that you have seen pray regularly? (Even the ministers and priests in TV shows hardly pray at all in front of the camera!) Of all the characters who have even occasionally prayed, few appear to be familiar with prayer, comfortable with it, knowledgeable about it.

We receive no training in prayer, we see no one modeling a prayer life for us, we have little societal support for prayer. As a consequence, even people who come to church to worship God are fuzzy about the duties of prayer.

This ignorance about prayer is tragic, really, when you consider that being aware of God's presence in prayer is one of the routine gifts that sustain life—like conversations with your best friend, or the sound of your children laughing. The irony of a life without prayer is that it forces a person to keep busy in order to cover up the fact that there isn't a point in doing anything! A life devoid of prayer will ultimately become a life devoid of peace.

And yet for the priest, prayer is not simply the way to peace. Prayer is also a responsibility. Even though prayer is the sustaining, inspiring force of every religious person's life, prayer is not something you *consume*—that is, something you do because it makes you feel good, like eating a hot fudge sundae. Prayer is a service, just as worship is a service. We pray not simply to God, but *for* God, in the sense of fulfilling God's requirement. "What does the LORD require of you but to do justice, and to love kindness, and to walk humbly with your God?" (Micah 6:8).

In the world at large, human beings are regarded primarily as consumers. And one characteristic of the consumer is that a consumer is nonresponsible. "The customer is always right," and it is the task of the seller to address the consumer's every need and whim. The only requirement placed on a consumer is to show up and spend. But when we, as fully human beings, enter the sanctuary to perform our priestly function, we become *responsible.* Each of us is a full human being in worship, an adult. We must put away the infantile behavior fostered by consumerism, and accept responsibility. And *the number-one responsibility we have as priests is prayer.*

It should also be noted that consumerism fosters not only a lack of responsibility, but also the anticipation of instant gratification. We are taught to expect immediate results from everything. So when we enter worship, either personal or corporate, we naturally expect to find prayer deeply sustaining and profoundly inspiring the first time, and *every* time, we pray. Need I point out that neither life nor prayer works that way? There are times when conversations, even with your best friend, are not pleasant; there are times when your children are not laughing; there are times when one does not feel God's presence in prayer. But your friend will remain your friend, if you have a soul; your children remain your children; and God remains God.

Prayer, like other responsibilities, demands discipline (a word remarkably rare in advertising). Just as one would not expect to sit down at a piano for the first time, and after a half hour's practice play Beethoven's *Moonlight Sonata,* so one should not expect to walk into church one day and in a half hour develop the spiritual awareness of a saint. It may happen; but for most of us, even small improvements take years. Thomas Merton, certainly one of the saints of the last century, says we always remain beginners.

Here, by the way, is yet another of the benefits of worshiping together. By establishing a time and place where we meet for

worship, we help discipline ourselves to pray—sort of like an
aerobics class for the soul.

The Five Duties of Prayer

Let us turn now to the specific priestly duties of prayer in the
worship service. There are four traditional types of prayer: (1)
Adoration and praise; (2) Confession of sin; (3) Thanksgiving;
and (4) Supplication and intercession. In seminary, we learned to
remember them with the acronym ACTS, as in the acts of God,
which we celebrate in worship.

When we come to consider not just *types* of prayers, but *duties*
of prayer, we must bear in mind that modern society has greatly
increased the need to properly prepare for worship. Not surpris-
ingly, we have duties from each of the four types of prayers listed
above, but the secular world has forced upon us a further duty—
the prayer of preparation. Prayers of preparation are not different
types of prayers from the others. In fact, they are made up of
varying amounts of adoration, confession, and so forth. Their
uniqueness derives from their function in the timetable of worship, as I hope the description below will make clear.

By the way, you will note that these prayer duties are no more
difficult to remember than the types of prayers, even though one
has been added. The new acronym now spells PACTS, as in the
pact God made with Moses, and the pact God made through
Jesus. To summarize, the duties of prayer in worship are:

> Preparation
> Adoration and praise
> Confession of sin
> Thanksgiving
> Supplication and intercession

Remember the PACTS we have with God, and you will remember your priestly prayer duties.

The First Prayer Duty: Preparation

The first duty is the prayer of preparation. I list prayer of preparation first not only because it comes at the beginning of worship,

but also because it is of first importance. The lack of proper preparation is the chief factor in the sterility of much modern worship. If we as priests do not take the time to close the sanctuary door to consumerism, it enters like the devil's own army, savagely devouring the soul of the congregation and leaving worshipers with the trite, conventional husk of a church service. No amount of arm-waving and passionate display on the part of the preacher will be able to breathe life into such a carcass of worship.

In order to function as a priest, you will have to enter the sanctuary of your soul, swing its massive doors shut against the flood of consumerism (and everything else), slowly and reverently penetrate into the silence of your cathedral, and pray. This is your preparation for the entire service of worship in the hour to come. Please understand the importance of preparation. If we do not properly prepare for worship at the beginning of the service, too large a part of every subsequent prayer will be devoted to recapturing worship as a mode of being, until the day comes when we go through an entire service without experiencing worship as a mode of being. Thus we will find ourselves cut off from the assurance of God in our midst, which I referred to above as the religious presence of mind.

When should we begin the prayer of preparation? The obvious answer is, just as we begin worship! It is pointless to prepare ourselves in silence and then immediately start chatting with our neighbor and greeting everyone around us. Worship must follow directly on the heels of preparation, or the preparation does little good. As we begin our prayer of preparation, all casual conversation and announcements should come to an end.

One of the best parts of Sunday mornings is greeting friends and acquaintances, swapping stories, seeing how everyone's getting along, sometimes kidding each other—genuine Christian fellowship. It is the proper way to gather for worship. But when we *are* gathered, we turn to the purpose of the gathering—honoring God.

Ideally, the organ (or other instrumental) prelude is the priest's clue to start a prayer of preparation. (This means, then, that the prelude should come *after* the greeting, announcements, and fellowship time.) The prelude should be followed by a period of silence (or quiet music; chimes, for instance) in which the prayer(s) are completed. If your worship service does not provide silence after the prelude, you will have to finish preparation during the prelude itself. If the prelude is followed by announcements or other interruptions, make a request that the structure of worship be changed slightly to allow you the opportunity to properly discharge your duty.

Don't be shy about speaking up on this subject. Remember that conversation with God requires our complete attention, which means bringing other conversations to a close. Would you ask time with your supervisor at work, and then stroll into your supervisor's office in a group, stand in front of her or him, and go on chatting with your friends? If your earthly supervisor is worthy of this much respect, how much more so is God.

The Great Commandment and the Prayer of Preparation. When the lawyer asked Jesus which commandment was the first of all, Jesus answered with not one, but *two* commandments: "You shall love the Lord your God with all your heart, and with all your soul, and with all your mind, and with all your strength. The second is this, 'You shall love your neighbor as yourself'" (Mark 12:30–31). Jesus refused to separate these commandments, because they just don't make any sense unless they're together. Asking Jesus which of these two commandments is really the first of all would be like asking, "Which of the wooden beams, the horizontal one or the vertical one, is really the cross?" Unless you have them both together, you don't have anything at all. So also our prayers of preparation, reflecting as they do our lives of obedience, will have two parts, which we will examine in turn.

The first part of a prayer of preparation, the "vertical" part, is designed to turn one's attention completely to God. It may take any one of several forms. It may, for instance, be printed in the bulletin. This practice has several advantages: It's easy for visitors to find; it provides a certain sense of togetherness, when all the priests know they're offering up the same prayer; it can even be spoken together. Its drawbacks include its length (ordinarily there isn't a lot of room in the bulletin) and inflexibility (perhaps closing the door to other more effective prayers of preparation).

If you bring your own Bible to worship, or if your sanctuary has Bibles in the pews, you will find many good vertical prayers of preparation in its pages. Here, for instance, are the opening lines of Psalm 104:

> Bless the LORD, O my soul. O LORD my God, you are very great. You are clothed with honor and majesty, wrapped in light as with a garment. You stretch out the heavens like a tent, you set the beams of your chambers on the waters, you make the clouds your chariot, you ride on the wings of the wind, you make the winds your messengers, fire and flame your ministers. (Ps. 104:1–4)

A second excellent source is your hymnbook. You will want to search your hymnbook for great hymns *addressed to God,* the words of which can be read in silence as a vertical prayer of preparation. Some hymns ("Amazing Grace," for instance) are more like statements of faith than prayers. They are in the third person, not the second, and so are not really directed to God. Look for hymns in the second person. If *you* or *thou* occurs in the hymn and refers to God, then you have a potential prayer of preparation, since the hymn is a conversation directly with God. ("How Great Thou Art" is a good example of a hymn that is also a prayer, and can be used for a prayer of preparation.) Perhaps the worship committee of your church could attach a list of those hymn numbers to the book itself.

On any given Sunday, the place to start looking for a hymn to offer as a vertical prayer of preparation is among the hymns you will be singing during the worship hour. By offering them first in silent prayer, you will grasp more clearly what it is that you are offering. It is possible to plan a worship service so that at least one of the listed hymns can double as a vertical prayer of preparation (a practice I find helpful in the preparation of sermons, too).

Here's a well-known hymn that makes a beautiful vertical prayer:

> Spirit of God, descend upon my heart.
> Wean it from earth, through all its pulses move
> Stoop to my weakness, mighty as thou art,
> And make me love thee as I ought to love.

Another way to provide printed vertical prayers of preparation is to tape various prayers of the ancients onto the blank page(s) at the end of your hymnbook (but be careful not to violate the copyright law). Here, for example, is a prayer of St. Anselm (1033–1109):

> Oh Lord our God, Grant us grace to desire Thee with our whole heart; that so desiring we may seek and find Thee; and so finding Thee may love Thee; and loving Thee, may hate those sins from which Thou has redeemed us. Amen.[1]

I would like to put in a plug here for memorizing scripture, in this particular case for use as a vertical prayer of preparation. I know the dangers of memorization—I have heard numbers of priests drone through the Lord's Prayer without the least thought to what they were saying. Many a worshiper would be shocked speechless if the petitions in the prayer being offered were actually granted. Nonetheless I also know that the Spirit moves beneath, as well as through, the words. And in the silence of the sanctuary, it is a blessing to close your eyes and let your spirit sweep over the Word of God:

> To you, O LORD, I lift up my soul.
> Oh my God, in you I trust;
> do not let me be put to shame;
> do not let my enemies exult over me.
> Do not let those who wait for you be put to shame;
> let them be ashamed who are wantonly treacherous.
> Make me to know your ways, O LORD;
> teach me your paths.
> Lead me in your truth, and teach me,
> for you are the God of my salvation;
> for you I wait all day long.
> Be mindful of your mercy, O LORD, and of your steadfast
>   love, for they have been from of old.
> Do not remember the sins of my youth or my transgressions;
>   according to your steadfast love remember me, for your
>   goodness' sake, O LORD!
>
>   (Ps. 25:1–7)

And the Second Is Like Unto It. . . . We come now to the second part of the prayer of preparation, the "horizontal," as in the horizontal beam of the cross (representing the commandment to love one's neighbor as oneself). The horizontal can be a little confusing because it involves directing our attention toward our neighbors while we are in silent prayer with God.

As I begin to prepare to worship God, I want to focus all my energies and attention in God's direction. This is not to say, however, that I try to block out awareness of the people sitting around me. On the contrary, as a priest I want to become *more* aware of them as I bring them to the throne of God. It may strike the beginner as a bit odd, but the joy of Christian fellowship actually deepens in the silence of the horizontal prayer of preparation, as each worshiper performs an act of love in lifting fellow worshipers into the fuller presence of God.

As priests, each of us has religious responsibilities for all the members of the worshiping congregation. Just as Jesus was unwilling to separate the commandment to love God with all the heart, mind, soul, and strength from the commandment to love one's neighbor as oneself, so we cannot separate our preparation, in fact our whole service of worship, from those around us. "Those who do not love a brother or sister whom they have seen, cannot love God whom they have not seen" (1 John 4:20). Thus each priest blesses the congregation with a horizontal prayer of preparation.

To keep the horizontal prayer "real," and not just theoretical, I recommend naming specific members of the congregation in prayer. A good place to begin is with people in your pew. Many churches have the custom of passing a friendship pad the length of the pew during the announcements, literally dropping into your lap the necessary information for the horizontal part of preparation. You don't have to remember every name, and you can even write down the name as the pad passes you, if your memory is (as a friend of mine describes hers) good, but short.

There are times in everyone's life when one's burden is so great that it drives thoughts of others' situations right out of one's mind. When you find yourself in this predicament, when you need time alone with God, take it. But you are indeed unfortunate if this condition prevails *every* Sunday morning of your life. Your

~~duty as a priest is to gather God's flock with you as you prepare~~
for worship. If you approach the throne alone, with no horizontal
prayer, you may be greeted as Cain was: "Where is your brother
Abel?" (Gen. 4:9).

The following is one suggestion for the form such a horizontal prayer might take.

> Lord, —(name)—, —(name)— and I come before you in love,
> with praise and thanksgiving for the gift of life today. Fill us
> all with the light of your presence, Eternal God of Grace, and
> grant each of us spiritual food for our journeys. Bind our
> hearts in Christian love, we ask in Jesus' name. Amen.

Your own prayer list (see below) will help you to select others for
this or a similar horizontal prayer.

Naturally, as we mature in faith, our spirit finds its own words
of preparation, and our hearts to a certain extent wordlessly prepare themselves. We must keep in mind, however, that preparation is so vitally important that we must not become complacent
about it. It is better to err on the side of deliberateness when
offering a prayer of preparation (by reading a printed prayer, for
instance) than to simply lean back in the pew, feeling "pretty
good about church." Proper preparation is a responsibility each
of us has to God and to every fellow worshiper.

The Second Prayer Duty: Adoration and Praise

These two terms—*adoration* and *praise*—are often used inter-
changeably. They certainly have enough in common to be treated
together here, centered as they are on the joy of knowing God.
Yet I find it helpful to maintain the ancient distinction between
them. Adoration is when love loses all restraints and judgment—
it is absolutely pure and cannot really be expressed in words.
Occasionally we experience adoration when looking at a sleep-
ing child, a magnificent landscape, or even the distant launching
of a space shuttle. We are only afterwards aware of a certain bliss
that surpasses both speech and thought. This awareness of real-
ity/state of being (the two dimensions cannot be separated) is
only a glimmer, or echo, of the soul's awareness of God. But ado-

ration of anything less than God is a fleeting thing—the child wakes up, you spot litter in the landscape, the shuttle deploys a military satellite. Only in worship may the soul fix itself on the Eternal Adored, the Creator God.

But this means that a prayer of adoration is not simply silent, but *wordless*. A lot of folks ("verbal" types—like most of us ministers, for instance!) often find themselves lost with respect to wordless prayers. So don't be discouraged if prayers of adoration don't come easily or quickly. If you diligently perform your priestly functions, they will come. Adoration is actually a state of contemplation, a state often not available to the beginning priest.

Praise, on the other hand, is putting emotions, perceptions, and beliefs into words (and often, music—see chapter 4). In the oldest hymnbook in our sanctuary—the book of Psalms—we are instructed at least 57 times to praise God.

> Praise the LORD! Praise the LORD from the heavens; praise him in the heights!
> Praise him, all his angels; praise him, all his host!
> Praise him, sun and moon; praise him, all you shining stars!
> Praise him, you highest heavens, and you waters above the heavens!
> (Ps. 148:1–4)

In the Reformed tradition, to which we Presbyterians belong, we put praise at the beginning of worship for two reasons. First, our praise is always praise of *God*; by beginning here, we declare that our worship, like our lives, centers on and revolves around God, not ourselves. Second, praise is an occasion for joy! And regardless of how well some of our worship services may disguise the fact, our chief purpose in life (and how much more, then, in worship) is to glorify and *enjoy* God forever!

The duty of praise is both exhilarating and easy, on most Sundays. Simply be aware of what you are saying (and singing); concentrate on the One you love, and you will fulfill this duty in worship.

The Third Prayer Duty: Confession

We Presbyterians customarily offer a prayer of confession of sin, usually printed in the bulletin, sometimes read from a worship

aid like the hymnbook. The idea behind confessing our sin is not
to make us feel miserable about ourselves, or to wallow in our
depravity. Rather we are simply putting into words the obvious,
namely that our *own* lives testify to the truth that "all have sinned
and fall short of the glory of God" (Rom. 3:23). The confession
clears the air between ourselves and God, who knows our sins
and shortcomings anyway; and it acknowledges the glory and
majesty of the eternally pure and righteous Lord in our midst.
Confession of sin is the humble admission that we are not God,
and at the same time a sign of the deep trust we have in God's
love. Filled with the assurance that God's love for us covers all
our sins, and at the same time aware that our righteousness
depends completely on God alone, we dare to launch into a confession of our true selves, with the same faith that allows a child
to leap from the side of the swimming pool into his mother's arms.

Young people in confirmation class have asked me, "Why
should I say the prayer of confession? I didn't do those things!"
It would be easy to chalk this feeling up to a desire to escape
blame (not all that uncommon among *adults* in church), but there
is also the question of integrity. Why should I stand before God
and say something I don't believe is true?

Why, indeed? There isn't a place on earth that lying accom-
plishes less than in the House of God. "The LORD does not see as
mortals see; they look on the outward appearance, but the LORD
looks on the heart" (1 Sam. 16:7). Can we fool God? Is God
pleased with empty or lying words? On the contrary, words that
have no root of truth in the heart are blown away like party con-
fetti in a hurricane. They count for less than nothing. Why, then,
say the prayer of confession?

There are many good reasons. First, it is our sin that cuts us off
from God, and nothing but confessing it leads to the forgiveness
that restores us. Second, by confessing each week, we acknowledge that we are naturally inclined to sin, and would be fooling
ourselves to imagine that we are "getting over it." True, "God . . .
gives us the victory through our Lord Jesus Christ" (1 Cor.
15:57), but the victory is not complete in this life, and to forget
that fact is to court foolishness.

Third, just repeating the prayer may bring to our minds otherwise forgotten sins and shortcomings, some of which may still need to be set right, and all of which need to be laid before God. Fourth, if the prayer is authentic for whoever wrote it, it will help cultivate a sense of repentance, trust, and humility in us, whether or not the specific examples of sin bear on our lives the past week. Fifth, it has always been true that people sin without being aware of it: "Who can detect their errors? Clear me from hidden faults" (Ps. 19:12). In our incredibly complex age, when the act of buying bath towels or orange juice carries with it hidden moral questions, we are in no great danger of *over*-confessing.

Sixth, the mature Christian accepts his or her connection to the sins of others, because all human beings are woven into a tight web. Would it surprise you to learn, on the day of judgment, that a missed opportunity for kindness on your part led directly to a murder somewhere else? Or that by ignoring a quiet young woman, you actually contributed to a teen pregnancy? Or that your cutting someone off in traffic accounted for a few of the blows felt by an abused child? You may be saying to yourself at this point something like, "What!? If I'm going to be held responsible for every ramification of every little thing I've done or haven't done, there's no way I can live a righteous life!" When you've realized this, you have taken the first step toward understanding the crucifixion. And repeating the prayer of confession makes a little more sense.

Finally, you are not confessing to human beings, who might not know you are innocent and might therefore judge you unjustly. You are confessing to God, as David did: "Against you, you alone, have I sinned" (Ps. 51:4). Recall that God looks upon the heart—your heart—and is quite capable of separating the wheat from the chaff. Let God judge just how much of the prayer applies to you.

If, after studying these perspectives, however, you still believe that prayer does not apply to you, do not say it. Present yourself in integrity before the Lord, as Job did. I believe that God will teach you what you need to know. May the lesson be merciful.

The Fourth Prayer Duty: Thanksgiving

The fourth duty of prayer is thanksgiving. It would seem almost unnecessary to point out our duty in this regard, since it is hard to imagine someone attending a worship service, under ordinary circumstances, without some sense of thanksgiving to God. Not only do we have much to be thankful for, but the act of thanking God is one of the great spiritual pleasures.

So a spirit of thanksgiving should pervade the service. Why then list it as a duty, and even recommend that at least one unison prayer of thanksgiving—either spoken or sung—be included in every worship service?

Once again we return to the fact that certain actions are demanded of us, among which is thanksgiving. "Enter [God's] gates with thanksgiving" (Ps. 100:4). It is not a responsibility that should be left up to chance, because it is not only a means of expressing our love of God, but the act itself actually increases the piety and devotion that true worship requires.

Another good reason to give thanks together is that the sheer force of unison thanksgiving will turn the hearts of some from their burdens to their blessings. It is easy to focus on the things that are going wrong. Thanksgiving helps to balance our perspective, by turning our attention to the things that are going right. "Though the wrong seems oft so strong, God is the ruler yet." Worship is the first place to remember that.

And there are times when life's wounds are so deep that thanksgiving is swept away from us. When a spouse (or a marriage) dies; when a career is lost; when one has stumbled deeply into sin and has received the sentence—at times like these thanksgiving does not come to the lips. At times like these, the *congregation's* act of giving thanks can spiritually carry someone through that dark night of the soul. The hope that our thanksgiving expresses may be a large part of the reason they are in church.

The Fifth Prayer Duty:
Supplication and Intercession

We come at long last to the duty most people think of when they think of prayer—asking God for something. Again for the sake of clarification, I will adopt a common distinction between the terms *supplication* and *intercession*. I will use the term *supplica-*

tion when referring to requests pertaining to ourselves; *intercession* will refer to prayers on behalf of other people.

Asking for something might not seem like a duty, but no law says a duty has to be unpleasant. It is a duty because we are instructed to do it: "Ask, and it will be given you; search, and you will find; knock, and the door will be opened for you. For everyone who asks receives, and everyone who searches finds, and for everyone who knocks, the door will be opened" (Matt. 7:7–8). One indication of the love of God is that the act of fulfilling God's commands is generally pleasant in itself. The psalmist says it this way: "The precepts of the LORD are right, rejoicing the heart . . . in keeping them there is great reward" (Ps. 19:8, 11). You've heard it said humorously many times: "It's a dirty job, but someone's got to do it!" You're a priest—you're that someone.

With regard to supplication (asking something for yourself), I have only this piece of advice: Go ahead and ask. I read and hear often that there are selfish things we shouldn't ask for. I can understand the sentiment behind this idea, but there are other considerations, too. First of all, in all honesty, we ought to be asking for what we really want. We can't fool God by pretending we don't want something. Show some spunk! Second, we ought to be trusting God to turn us down if it's not best in the long run (as Paul learned in 2 Corinthians 12:8–9). Third, it is quite possible to think a request is selfish, when God would be happy to grant it. It was wildly selfish of Bartimaeus to request his eyesight, but Jesus granted his petition (Mark 10:46–52). Even Jesus himself, "tempted in every way as we are, yet without sin" (Heb. 4:15), asked God to remove the "cup" (the suffering of the crucifixion). This is not to say that your every request will be granted. (Even Jesus' request was not.) But you *are* a child of God; God *does* love you. Go ahead and ask.

With regard to intercessory prayer (praying for others), here are some suggestions concerning the worship service:

1. Keep a written prayer list. It doesn't have to be elaborate—it isn't going into any archives. Use the back of your calendar if you want to, or the margin of your checkbook register, or the insert to the bulletin. If you're a methodical person, get a little pocket notebook. Use

the list at home, during the worship service for "flash" prayers, and for the formal prayers of supplication and intercession (for example, pastoral prayer, prayers of the people).

2. Space your requests—don't just rattle off a list of names. Take the time to think about each person on your list.

3. Visualize yourself putting a hand on their shoulder or taking them by the arm to Christ. You may not be able to do it physically, but the closer you can come in the mind's eye, the better. I realize that this kind of prayer will make you more vulnerable. It strengthens ties with suffering people, so that you feel their pain more. But keep in mind that you'll be spending eternity with them, and no prayer of love is ever lost or forgotten.

Conclusion

I hope I haven't dropped too much of a load on you in this chapter. If you picked up this book not being aware that you were a priest, you may be feeling a bit overwhelmed with all these duties—and there are still four chapters of duties to go! The actual "activities" associated with the priestly duties of prayer—reading a prayer of preparation, keeping a prayer list, and so forth—are neither strenuous nor particularly time-consuming. You may be performing many, or all, of them already. It's just that they must be done, and *you can do it!* In the words of Jesus, "Take my yoke upon you, and learn from me; for I am gentle and humble in heart, and you will find rest for your souls. For my yoke is easy, and my burden is light" (Matt. 11:29–30).

Furthermore, the worship service should be *designed* so that you don't have to think too much about whether you will be fulfilling your duties. You should be able to take a bulletin and put a *1* beside an opportunity for preparation, a *2* beside an opportunity for adoration and praise, a *3* beside an opportunity for confession, and so forth. Thus you will know that if you simply follow the order of worship, every opportunity you need—for *all* the duties of prayer—will arise in due course. Don't hesitate to speak up if the regular worship does not provide these opportunities.

REVIEW QUESTIONS

1. What is the chief responsibility of the priest?
2. List the five duties of prayer.
3. Why are prayers of preparation so important?
4. What are the two parts of the prayer of preparation?
5. Why is the hymn "How Great Thou Art" better suited to be a vertical prayer of preparation than the hymn "Amazing Grace"?
6. List five benefits of a prayer of confession.
7. Obtain a Sunday bulletin and identify opportunities for each of the five duties of prayer during worship.

DISCUSSION QUESTIONS

1. How do you prepare for worship?
2. What are the strengths of your worship service?
3. Write a sample horizontal prayer of preparation and share it.
4. How does prayer in Sunday worship strengthen your devotion?
5. When, during worship, are you personally most likely to be aware of God's presence?

Chapter 4

The Duties of the Priest: Music

Be filled with the Spirit, as you sing psalms and hymns and spiritual songs among yourselves, singing and making melody to the Lord in your hearts.
—Ephesians 5:18–19

*T*here is nothing quite like music for opening up the soul to God. Music is a duty in worship for the same reason that prayer, offering, and study are duties—God commands it and God enjoys it. We are, after all, serving the living God in worship. That is our job. Certainly one of the perks of our job is the religious presence of mind, the awareness that we are in the presence of the Holy Spirit. And nowhere in the service is the presence of the Holy Spirit more obvious than in the corporate discipline of making "a joyful noise to God" (Ps. 66:1).

The natural response of experiencing the Spirit is joy— as our sense of God's presence increases, so does our desire to make a joyful noise. Thus we experience a spiralling effect. Joy produces music; music, in turn, produces joy, which then produces more music. I am convinced that the truest measure of spiritual vitality in a congregation is the level of energy that the congregation devotes to its hymns.

Music—congregational music—has been a part of the Judeo-Christian tradition for millennia. According to Exodus, when the Israelites had safely passed through the sea and escaped from the Egyptians, Miriam, the sister of Moses, commanded the people to "Sing to the LORD, for he has triumphed gloriously" (15:21). Thus congregational music dates from the very origin of our religious heritage.

It is clear, also, that as the tradition developed, so did the role of music. The oldest hymnbook in our tradition, the biblical book of Psalms, contains many commands to make music to God: "Sing praises to the LORD" (Ps. 9:11); "Sing praises to the LORD, O you his faithful ones, and give thanks to his holy name" (30:4); "Praise the LORD with the lyre; make melody to him with the harp of ten strings. Sing to him a new song" (33:2–3); "Shout to God with loud songs of joy. Sing praises to God, sing praises" (47:1, 6); "Make a joyful noise to God, all the earth; sing the glory of his name" (66:1); "Sing to God, sing praises to his name; lift up a song to him who rides upon the clouds" (68:4); "Sing aloud to God our strength . . . Raise a song, sound the tambourine, the sweet lyre with the harp. Blow the trumpet" (81:1–3). The whole book of Psalms culminates in a thunderous call to music—the last six psalms (145–150) all ring with the command to worship God in song. In response, beyond our hearing, the universe is filled with "the voice of a great multitude, like the sound of many waters and like the sound of mighty thunderpeals, crying out, 'Hallelujah! For the Lord our God the Almighty reigns. Let us rejoice and exult and give him the glory' " (Rev. 19:6–7).

It is thrilling to be a part of the great choir of the universe every Sunday morning during worship, and the cost of admission to that choir is nothing more than singing God's praise with passion. All of us have experienced the thrill at some time or other, in some moment of worship, as our voices join together in such inspiring offerings as "How Great Thou Art," "Christ the Lord is Risen Today," and "Joyful, Joyful, We Adore Thee." So much of our spiritual life, our religious presence of mind—the thanksgiving, the comfort, the elation, the love—is wrapped up in our music. "That the singing of spiritual hymns is a goodly thing and pleasing to God, I do not think is hidden from any Christian. . . ."[1] Congregational singing is one more duty that generally returns far more than it costs. God has struck a good deal with us!

There are, no doubt, great and noble ways to love God, great and noble ways to be obedient to God. How effective will we be in those instances, though, if we ignore such a simple, practical way of being loving and obedient as singing a hymn?

Make a Joyful Noise—
in Spite of Your Conditioning

Next to prayer, music is probably the most neglected priestly duty in many Presbyterian worship services. And while we seem to respond quickly to prayer training, progress is slower with regard to our music duties. I am convinced that this deficiency can be traced to unwanted influence from the culture in which we live. Unfortunately, this cultural influence has the effect of contaminating and weakening the one thing above all others that should remain pure and strong—our offering of worship to God each Sunday.

In the world at large, there is now, and has been for some time, a tidal wave of specialization in every field of human endeavor. You may recall the story of the man who went to the clinic to get something for a cold. He asked the young doctor, "Are you a general practitioner?" "No," the doctor replied, "I specialize." "Oh," said the man, "ear, nose, and throat?" "Well," said the doctor, "my area of specialization is the nose." The man pondered this for a moment, then asked, "Which nostril?"

Somehow this story was funnier twenty years ago, partly because we felt like poking fun at the sea of specialization that seemed to be engulfing our world. Now we simply take specialization for granted.

The field of music is also extremely specialized. Singing is left to the "professionals," and if you're not particularly good at carrying a tune, there's a whole lot of pressure on you not to sing at all, but simply to listen to someone else sing. When you stand in church, you may feel embarrassed to sing out, or even embarrassed when a member of your family sings out. Culture determines what's "cool," and singing out isn't cool.

So music is an area in which simply doing your duty in worship can be a wonderfully liberating experience. You are not only free to sing loud in church, it is required and expected of you. You will find that singing the hymns with gusto, while requiring some courage, actually strengthens your love for God, increases the pleasure of worship, and gives you a sense of your own personal power.

Musical Persons and Musicians

Specialization in the field of music has created the false idea that "musical" people are people who can carry a tune. This is nonsense. Virtually every human being is musical. Some, due to training, inclination, and natural gifts, can *articulate* the music better than others. These folks are called "musicians."

Let me make the distinction clear. You are a *musical person* if you enjoy music, if music "speaks" to you. You are a musical person if you ever hum along with a song on the radio, or tap out the beat with a dance band, or break into an old tune when you're feeling good, or own a stereo system, or sing in the shower, or have a favorite song. You are a musical person if you can tell the difference between the tunes of "The Star Spangled Banner" and "Happy Birthday."

You are a *musician* if you can carry a tune, read music, play an instrument, and so forth. Congregational singing is designed not simply for musicians, but for *every* musical person. Otherwise, why have the whole congregation do it? Why not leave it all for the chancel choir? But God has made you musical so that you might be a part of the *congregational* choir.

The *musician* must constantly struggle against temptation in worship—the temptation to sing for narcissistic reasons (to hear the sound of his or her own voice, and/or to win the admiration of others). And for the gifted musician, this can really be a problem, especially if the congregation keeps asking you to sing. But the musical person who is *not* a musician sings only for spiritual reasons—in the case of worship, to love and glorify God. Thus, you have all the more reason to sing out if you can't carry a tune, because God recognizes your act as pure devotion.

Nobody is listening to judge how well you sing in worship. When we enter the sanctity of God's house to offer our praises, we draw an imaginary line around the building. Those who judge have to wait out in the parking lot. Seriously, in the holiness of worship, all negativity is suspended and we are really set free to love God.

I once had the good fortune to serve a church in which neither the senior pastor, nor the clerk of session, nor the youth group

Sunday school teacher could carry a tune in a bucket. The three
of them share the same first name; for the sake of protecting their
privacy, I'll identify them all as "Phil." They knew it—they even
joked about it. Yet each Sunday morning, the three Phils were up
there, one in the chancel area, the other two in the first few rows,
singing out to the glory of God. Their lack of self-consciousness,
their sense of devotion and duty, were as inspirational to the congregation as the finest voices of the choir—and that choir has
some very fine voices!

So if you sing off key, sing loud! The measure of a congregation's devotion is better gauged by its "joyful noises" than by the
more culturally acceptable forms of music.

The Purpose of Congregational Singing

If only certain people are musicians, what is the purpose of *congregational* singing? Why does God require of us a song?

A conversation with church musicians and pastors will turn up
many reasons. Here are a few:

1. Music has great power to express how we feel. If we
   truly love God, truly glorify God, we are driven to
   music. Mere words are not enough. To borrow from a
   popular song of a few years ago, "I have to say 'I love
   you' in a song."
2. Music teaches us better than simply reading words. In
   the words of Basil, fourth-century bishop of Caesarea:
   "[The Holy Spirit] adds the grace of music to the truth
   of doctrine. Charmed by what we hear, we pluck the
   fruit of the words without realizing."[2]
3. Music, in expressing our passion for God, strengthens
   the faith of the other priests with whom we worship.
   (Take another look at Eph. 5:19; and remember the
   three Phils.) Even without being aware of it, fellow
   worshipers pick up on the joy and faithfulness of our
   singing. When we recall that as priests we have the
   duty to "build one another up in love," this dimension
   of music gains in importance.
4. Your singing greatly inspires the pastor. I have
   preached in dozens of churches, and the single greatest

source of uplift in worship has been the congregational singing. When there is no spirit in the singing, why should the congregation expect spirit in the preaching? On the other hand, when I hear strong congregational singing, I know the Spirit is at home in the sanctuary, and the congregation is both sincere and prepared to hear the sermon. What crumbs I have assembled in the study now seem like a feast for royalty, and, as the psalmist says, "My heart overflows with a goodly theme" (Ps. 45:1).

5. The last purpose I will list for the priestly duty of congregational singing is the most spiritual, and by far the most important. In music, as in communion, we are lifted into the presence of God as one body, and in our own simple and ordinary way, we experience the aura of heaven in the sanctuary of our local church. We are linked to believing Christians everywhere, those who have preceded us and those who are yet to come. In fact, when John "heard what seemed to be the voice of a great multitude, like the sound of many waters and like the sound of mighty thunderpeals, crying out, 'Hallelujah! For the Lord our God the Almighty reigns,'" what he was listening to, in part, was your own congregation, singing a song we all have yet to learn.

In the words of John Chrysostom, bishop of Constantinople:

Young and old, rich and poor, women and men, slaves and free, all sang one single melody . . . All the inequalities of social life are here banished. Together we make up a single choir in perfect equality of rights and of expression whereby earth imitates heaven. Such is the noble character of the Church.[3]

The Anthem

If I have established with you the critical importance of congregational singing (by all musical Christians, not just the musicians), let me take up for a moment the role of the anthem in the service of God.

In the game of football, eleven members of a team are involved in any one play, but there is only one football. When a team scores a touchdown, very few members of the team actually touch the ball during that play. Normally, even on a touchdown pass, only three people—the center, who snaps the ball to the quarterback; the quarterback; and the receiver—get their hands on the ball. The other eight team members on the field for that play never touch it.

However (and this is a big "however"), on a well-designed and executed play, *every* member of the team contributes to the touchdown. Some team members prevent the opponents from tackling the quarterback, so that he has a chance to throw the pass. Others mislead the defenders into believing that the pass is intended for them. Still others may block members of the opposing team who are trying to tackle the receiver after he has caught the ball. The odds of completing the play successfully *without* the help of everyone on the team are vanishingly small. The crowd may be cheering the one who crosses the goal line with the football in his hand, but the one who crosses the goal line with the football in his hand is cheering his teammates, without whom he never would have scored.

Being a worshiping member of the congregation puts you on the same worship "team" as the choir. You may not be singing while the choir offers God the anthem, and to the untrained eye and ear, you may not seem to have any role in it. But your role is critical in the work of the choir. Without your knowledgeable participation in worship, the anthem falls from the realm of the sacred to the realm of the secular. The choir's offering becomes merely entertainment.

Offering vs. Entertainment

Often, when deciding where the choir should stand to sing, what anthems are appropriate for a particular worship service, or whether props (including handheld microphones) are fitting, a discussion emerges as to whether the anthem is an offering to God or entertainment for the congregation.

Worship is work for *God*; that's why we're in church. We can entertain ourselves on our own time. Imagine how you would feel if you walked into a fast-food restaurant, and the person behind the counter, instead of waiting on you, cranked up his or her portable CD player to listen to a popular song for three or four minutes. Yet we do something similar when we turn from waiting on God to please ourselves with an anthem. We are in worship to wait on God, not to entertain ourselves.

But, you may ask, can't our music be pleasing to us, too? And what is the difference between sacred offering and entertainment, anyway?

First things first. Certainly God's music can and should be pleasing to us. But the music that is pleasing to *God* in worship (our first priority) will have one defining characteristic: It will give us a sense of the Divine. God commands worship in order to draw us near. Activities that take us in any other direction are a violation of the Sabbath.

I like different styles of music—pop, rhythm and blues, classical, Dixieland jazz. But not all music links me spiritually to God. "Boogie Woogie Bugle Boy from Company B" or "There's a Hole in the Bottom of the Sea" are not avenues to the Mystery.

What choral music is such an avenue? Music that:

1. Directs the attention toward God; often it is a setting of scripture itself.
2. Reflects, on some level, the depth (both of sorrow and of joy) of human life.
3. Shares God's passion for altruistic love and unqualified justice.
4. Seems timeless, as if our ancestors and our descendants could sing it with us.
5. Speaks not for one individual, but for the whole community of the church.

Many styles of music can meet these criteria. When they do, they make an offering fragrant and acceptable to God.

When does offering degenerate into entertainment? Well, simply put, it's when it is sung to the congregation instead of to God. Here are some signs: (1) eye contact with (and worse, gesturing to) individual members of the congregation; (2) elaborate or unusual dress; (3) idiosyncratic behavior (such as cradling a microphone as a stage entertainer would); (4) bowing after the performance; (5) excessive anxiety over the quality of the performance. To paraphrase Mark 7:23: "All these things come from within, from the hearts of the choir, and they defile an anthem."

The fact that the anthem is not designed to entertain the congregation, but to offer the congregation's spirit to God, means that certain behaviors are more appropriate for choir members. Those behaviors are as follows: (a) keep your eyes on the director; (b) wear robes (or similar simple dress if robes are not available); (c) move only in concert with the rest of the choir; (d) be seated quietly following the anthem; and (e) trust God to accept your offering, and let it go!

Anthem Responsibilities for the Congregation

Even if you do not sing in the choir, you are on the same worship team as the choir. You have responsibilities vis-à-vis the anthem before, during, and after the choir's offering.

First and most important, pay careful attention to your prayer and music duties. By so doing, you will help to create an atmosphere of worship from which the choir draws inspiration, and to which it adds its own dimension. If you and the congregation around you experience worship as a mode of being throughout the service, the anthem will naturally find its place in the gathered offering to God. The piety of the congregation is the soil from which the flower of the anthem springs.

Second, if it is possible to obtain the words to the anthem prior to its offering, read through them just as you would to prepare for the hearing of the scripture. Often the music director and pastor work in concert to plan weeks in advance, so there may well be some way for the congregation to study the words to upcoming anthems.

Third, get to know your music director and at least some members of the choir. The more personal our ties, the easier it is for us to understand how faith is motivating the music. Somehow we are more aware *as friends* of our common purpose in worshiping God than we are if we remain strangers.

Fourth, during the singing of the anthem, you should listen as intently as you do to the sermon, but with a different part of your mind. Intuitively, without much conscious thought, you should be able to locate that part of your soul that the choir, through the anthem, is pouring out to God. Ride along with the choir on the wings of the music.

If you find yourself distracted from the anthem for any reason, here are three little words that should help you listen: *close your eyes.* (Note that I am not recommending this as a way of listening to the *sermon,* so don't bother highlighting the previous sentence and showing it to me after I preach.) Seriously, you're perfectly safe in the sanctuary—you aren't likely to be hit by a car while sitting in your pew—so don't be afraid to shut down one sense in order to enhance another. If a dog runs across the front of the sanctuary with Mrs. Jones's hat in its mouth, you will have missed something by closing your eyes; but you'll miss something far more important if seeing with your eyes distracts you from seeing with your soul.

Finally, when the choir has been particularly inspiring, you will naturally want to share with the director and members after the service the joy that you have experienced. *How* you express yourself helps to shape the musicians' understanding of worship. "You sounded great!" puts the focus on the performer. "What a beautiful offering to God!" says "Thanks for giving God what I would love to give myself. You did me a wonderful favor, and I was right there with you!" Helping to keep their focus on God allows musicians to develop spiritually, which in turn benefits the whole congregation and deepens every worship service.

So, you are not a spectator in the stands when the choir sings. You are a teammate of the people making that particular musical offering. The choir's offering is therefore a part of your offering. You will feel a part of the best anthems. You will draw closer to the choir as you acknowledge that they have put into music what you would like to convey to God yourself.

Passing on the Gift

Since God loves and appreciates music, every priest should not only make music himself or herself, but encourage others to offer

their best, also. I am thinking here of children who may be growing up in your congregation as musicians, yet they are unheard
and unseen. It is cruel stupidity to *demand* that a child sing, especially while standing in the front of the sanctuary facing the congregation. But if a child is not developing musical gifts because
he or she lacks the opportunity, can't afford lessons or an instrument, doesn't sense any support within the church, or doesn't
realize what a beautiful gift his or her music would be to God, do
something about that. Start a children's choir. If your congregation has children who are instrumentalists, find a place in the
service for them to play. Play an instrument yourself as a role
model (or cajole another adult into doing it). Play a duet with
them or organize an ensemble. Ask them to sing or play regularly.
Start a scholarship fund to underwrite the cost of lessons. They
won't be young twice. By supporting a young person who is
developing as a musician, you will have extended your own praise
to God through another generation, even while you are opening
up a broad and wonderful spiritual path for a young person.

Getting Down to Specifics

The duties of the priest—every priest—with respect to music in
worship can be distilled into one line: "Make a joyful noise to
God." Sing. That's it. That is your duty. You may be a musician
and want to sing all day. You may be musical but not a musician,
and a bit uncomfortable singing when someone else can hear
you. Regardless of your musicality, God enjoys your effort. Only
good can come of it. Sing.

While you have but one *duty,* I would like to offer you the following *suggestions* to enrich your experience and enlarge the
benefits of your efforts. (These suggestions apply to all—musicians and musical persons alike.)

> 1. *Buy a hymnbook and get to know it.* Even if you can't
>   play or sing a note, a good hymnbook is an excellent
>   devotional book. You will benefit greatly by reading
>   through hymns during daily or weekly devotions. In
>   addition, your hymnbook may contain prayers, creeds,

and/or scripture readings that will stretch you spiritually. Your music director can show you how to use the indices in the back.

2. *Preview the hymns for Sunday morning's worship.* In your preparation time on Sunday morning, read through the hymns for the service. Singing a hymn to God without first reading the words is like giving your friend a gift that you never took out of the package to make sure it was what you ordered. "Sing ye praises with understanding" (Ps. 47:7 KJV). When you sing a hymn in worship, you are not a machine grinding out music to God. You are a human being. It makes a world of difference that you comprehend what you're singing.

3. *Stand or sit up straight when you sing, and breathe deeply.* Breath and *spirit* are the same word in the languages Jesus knew and spoke, so to sing with deep, powerful breath is to sing with deep, powerful spirit.

4. *Memorize a few hymns.* Memorization is vastly underrated in our generation as a spiritual tool. Many of us are old enough to see how far the pendulum has swung with respect to memorization! Next to scripture itself, hymns return the most benefit from the work of memorization. Carry a hymnbook in your mind, and you will be able to draw from it as needed.

5. *Ask to sing hymns and spiritual songs that you like, and occasionally learn a new one.* I am a great believer in having a repertoire. As a member of the congregation, you should be familiar with fifty or so good hymns, and you should do most of your singing from that repertoire. A word of caution here to musicians: Even if you can sight-read the most difficult hymns, it is *repetition* that mines the deepest meaning from music. Don't be in a hurry to sing a new hymn each week. Keep in mind also that those around you who are not musicians will struggle to derive *any* meaning from a hymn until they are moderately familiar with how it goes. This may take a while.

At least once a year—no matter what your age or musical ability—you should add a new hymn or song to your list (Ps. 96:1; 98:1; 149:1).

Conclusion

Your priestly duties with respect to music aren't all that numerous or complicated. Just sing. Be aware of what you are singing, why you are singing, to whom you are singing, and with whom you are singing. Here is a duty that can be a pure joy and a great boost on your spiritual journey. (And they call this work!)

REVIEW QUESTIONS

1. How can you sum up your music responsibilities in worship?
2. What is the difference between a musical person and a musician?
3. What benefits can you derive from owning a hymnbook?
4. List ways you can promote the spiritual growth of children through music.
5. Why should you read through Sunday morning's hymns before singing them?
6. What are five purposes for congregational singing?
7. Why is it natural to have both a hymn and the anthem during the offering portion of Sunday morning worship?

DISCUSSION QUESTIONS

1. On a scale of 1 to 10, with 1 being "musical person," and 10 being "musician," where would you rate yourself?
2. What are your three most favorite hymns? Any idea why they are your favorites?
3. How many indices does your hymnbook contain? How many do you know how to use? Is there anyone in your class who could show you how to use another of the indices?
4. Do you know the names of any young musicians in your congregation? How are they involved in worship? How might they be?
5. Find a hymn that is addressed directly to God (second person, grammatically) and decide when such a prayer would be appropriate. Offer the hymn at that appropriate time.

Chapter 5

The Duties of the Priest: Scripture and Sermon

*[My word] shall not return to me empty, but it shall accomplish
that which I purpose.*

—Isaiah 55:11

*N*othing has so characterized the Presbyterian expression
of Christian worship as the preaching of the Word. It was
through the preaching of Paul and the other apostles that
God spread the church across the Mediterranean world in
the first century of the current era; it was through the
preaching of Martin Luther that God lit the Reformation; it
was through the preaching of John Knox that Scotland
became home to Presbyterianism; it was through the
preaching of Francis Mackemie and other missionaries that
our tradition took root in America. And preaching is still the
most prominent feature of the Sunday morning worship.
Where can you look to find the living presence of God without
finding two essential ingredients—scripture and preachers?
Scripture interpreted is, for the Presbyterian, the continuing
revelation of God. God is hidden from our eyes, but sermon
(in concert with Bible study, as in daily devotionals) provides a window into the Mystery.

It troubles me greatly that, in so many pulpits and pews,
a dead, materialistic, analytical approach toward scripture
has displaced the lively approach of faith. In the analytical
approach, scripture is cold, dead words, which can be
mined for their one meaning. Faith, on the other hand, recognizes that God may use a passage of scripture today to
address an issue, to challenge or comfort us; but since
tomorrow is another day, God may use the *same* scripture
tomorrow *for an entirely different purpose.* Or God can
direct us to *another* passage of scripture to address the same

issue, a passage that we may never before have realized could pertain to the question at hand. It is best, and most accurate, according to faith, to consider the words themselves as living, as springing to life when read and reflected upon, as being inspired by the Spirit to move and change us.

The analyst imagines that God had one purpose, and one purpose only, in inspiring the writers of the Bible. If the scripture will only hold still, the analyst can figure out what God's purpose was 2,000 years ago when the scriptures were written (a purpose, apparently, that hasn't changed in two millennia, while human culture has experienced a minor adjustment or two). Listening to an analyst discuss a passage of scripture summons to my mind the image of a veterinarian who can't get a dog to hold still to extract something from the dog's throat. So the vet shoots the dog dead and then is able to extract the foreign object. What good is a dead dog? What good is dead scripture?

Preaching is not archaeology. It isn't as if we have dug up ancient instructions that some dead man left us 2,000 years ago, so that we can now listen to a properly trained scientist decipher those instructions. Preaching is the Holy Spirit's fanning of scripture into a flame that warms, tests, and refines its hearers. Preaching breathes life into scripture. In the words of Thomas Cartwright, English Puritan and professor at Cambridge, "As the fire stirred giveth more heat, so the Word, as it were, blown by preaching, flameth more in the hearers than when it is read."[1]

The Priest as Listener

Though it may seem, on certain occasions, that the efforts of the preacher have obscured, rather than revealed, what God would have us know in a particular moment, it is through preaching that the will of God unfolds for believers. Preaching is the momentary explosion of scripture, the experience of the Holy Spirit made audible, understandable, timely. Preaching is far more than one person's commentary on scripture; preaching is the unfolding of scripture into our lives in the moment of hearing. It is for this reason that the first Protestants thought of scripture and sermon as a unity.

The presence of the Holy Spirit, linking scripture and preaching, has significant consequences for the priest in the pew. First of all, preaching is the priest's encounter with God. Somewhere in the experience of preaching—the thoughts, the argument, the illustrations, the gestures, the tone of voice, the personal history shared between speaker and listener, the relationships fanning out from the hearer to his or her fellow worshipers, even the lights and pews and shape of the building—somewhere in all that the living God speaks to the people of God. If you are listening only for a point, or an interesting idea, that's all you will hear. You will have listened to God as you listen to a history lecture. You will have listened as an unbeliever, not as a priest.

To listen as a priest is to tune your whole being to the sermon, the way the priests at Delphi tuned themselves to the wind in the sacred oak. All human beings live in the same Mystery and seek guidance from it. It is, after all, a word from the same God, which is sought from all oracles by all priests. The only advantage of the Christian priest—and it is huge—is that we realize that the Word became flesh and dwelt among us, "and we have beheld his glory, glory as of the only Son of the Father" (John 1:14). We Presbyterians have intellectualized the sermon too much; we can learn from other priests. A sermon may be *composed* of words from a preacher; but it *conveys* a word from God. It isn't just our tradition that makes the sermon sacred. The sermon's sanctification is the timely work of the Holy Spirit.

Let me interject here that the sacredness of preaching does not translate one-to-one as sacredness of the preacher. Paul, speaking for all priests (which includes all preachers), said, "We have this treasure in earthen vessels, to show that the transcendent power belongs to God and not to us" (2 Cor. 4:7). The priest in the pulpit, like the priests in the pews, is certainly an "earthen vessel." It is the inspiration of God that creates the voice of God in the sermon.

Sometimes I wonder how anyone can take credit for any truly creative endeavor, most of all preaching. I cannot tell you how often I have been surprised at what God brings forth from my word processor in the preparation of a sermon. If I did not believe in the inspiration of the Holy Spirit, I would have *absolutely no idea* where my sermons come from—a fact that makes writing a sermon a very humbling experience. If God chooses not to speak, I have nothing to say (even though I may spend twenty minutes saying it, anyway).

In any event, preaching is far more than entertainment, even more than teaching. Preaching is opening up the oracle, and it marks the beginning of your work as interpreter of the oracle of God (one of the traditional priestly functions). As you listen for the breath of God in the breath of the preacher, you experience the excitement and responsibility of the priesthood. Your own spiritual journey, and the journeys of those whose lives will intertwine with yours in the coming week, rest in large part on your reception of the Word.

The second significant truth of the relationship between scripture, preaching, and priest is that you are not only interpreter, but also translator. The scripture lives in your life; the Holy Spirit moves through you on Monday, Tuesday—the whole week. This is one of the chief ways in which God is present in your community. To use a theological term, you become the *incarnation* of the Word. The Word first became flesh in Jesus; and today, in some way, or to a certain extent, the Word becomes flesh in you. You not only *interpret* the scripture for those around you, you also *translate* the scripture into action, behavior, attitude, the whole rhythm of life. You are in Christ, and Christ is in you.

Sunday Morning Duties

Your duties with respect to scripture and sermon are largely— one might say exclusively—designed to reflect and make visible the truth about these gifts as outlined above. Let's now explore the seven duties of interpretation.

The First Duty of Interpretation: Preparation

Insofar as possible, read the scripture *before* worship. If your preacher follows a lectionary, the scripture lessons are available in advance indefinitely. If not, many preachers will publish in the bulletin or newsletter the scriptures they have chosen for upcoming Sundays. Reading the scripture in advance significantly increases your opportunity to experience the religious presence of mind. The intrepretation of scripture begins with your reading, and is cross-fertilized by the reading and sermon in the worship service.

Suggestion: Let Sunday's scripture form the core of family worship on Saturday. Try to second-guess the preacher. What sounds important to you? There are no wrong answers; there is really no telling where God is leading us, until we get there. See who, among your family and friends, can think of the most related verses of scripture. Who can create a story or background for the passage? Who can think of an instance when it was, or could be, applied? You are not trying to complete something here, but only to open doors.

The Second Duty of Interpretation:
Pray for the Preacher

Pray for the preacher. Have a little morning devotional before you leave home for worship, or just add a word of prayer for the preacher to the grace you say before breakfast. Something like, "Lord, open our pastor's heart and soul to your word this morning, and inspire our pastor with your presence." Howard Rice writes, "Church members who pray for their preacher regularly are a part of the preaching process."[2]

A theme that we will have occasion again and again to return to is the fact that the preaching of the Word is a living, timely event. This morning's sermon comes at a certain point in the congregation's spiritual journey, and neither the sermon nor the point in the journey will ever come again. The presence of God's Spirit in the moment is critical. Ask God to bestow it upon the preacher.

You are praying for yourself when you pray for the preacher, because you, in your turn, must become the incarnation of the scripture. The sermon is the beginning of the work of scripture in you, and you want to get off to a good start. The clearer and more compelling the sermon, the more momentum *you* carry into *your* task. A good sermon makes your job easier. For this reason, it is wise to include a request that God clear your mind and open your heart to the meaning of that morning's scripture. (This request may be made in the morning when you rise; or during the prayer of preparation, or the confession of sin, or the prayer for illumination—you have many opportunities!)

The Third Duty of Interpretation: Honor the Bible

Honor the Bible in your sanctuary. One of the congregational preparations for worship is to open the Bible. This is done to indicate that the worship service is built upon the Word of God; that the living God's Word is new today; and that one chief reason for gathering to worship is to hear God speak.

In the Reformed tradition, we believe that only the presence of the Holy Spirit makes possible the correct understanding of scripture. This truth is often symbolized by flanking the sanctuary Bible with candles. Their flames represent the tongues of fire of the Spirit, hovering above the words, illuminating the mind to understand the Word. Another way of recognizing the need for the presence of the Holy Spirit is to preface the scripture reading with a prayer for illumination.

If there are candles beside the Bible representing the inspiration of the Holy Spirit, they should be lit as the Bible is opened. To avoid bibliolatry (that is, the idolatry of worshiping the *Bible* as a substitute for the worshiping of the *God* of the Bible), the opening and the candlelighting may be done just prior to the scripture reading, instead of at the very beginning of the service. Some churches close the Bible at the end of the service. Others leave it open to indicate its continued influence in the life of the congregation. As a priest, you have a responsibility to be aware of how the Bible is treated during worship.

The Fourth Duty of Interpretation: Honor Scripture

Honor scripture. That is, make preparation for the actual moment of the reading in the worship service. The French Reformed congregations stood to receive the gospel, adopting as tradition the reception accorded to scripture in Nehemiah 8:5. Whether your congregation stands to receive the scripture or not, you can look forward and plan ahead, so you're not fumbling with your purse through the first three verses.

The Fifth Duty of Interpretation: Listen to Scripture

Pay attention to the reading of the scripture. If you have honored scripture properly, you are relaxed and attentive before the first word of scripture is read. This is important, because just as the sermon is an integral part of the scripture, so the scripture is an integral part of the sermon. The pastor has written the bulk of the sermon, and there are times when all of us pastors suffer from a lack of inspiration. But God is always inspired. The first part of every sermon—that is, the *scripture* part—is written by God and is always good. So pay particular attention to God's opening remarks.

Even if you have read the scripture before coming to worship, you will notice that the minister or lay leader reads it differently than you did, stressing different words, conveying different ideas. This will not only show you the way scripture can convey many different truths, but also prepare you to hear the sermon.

The Sixth Duty of Interpretation: Listen to the Sermon

Pay attention to the preaching of the sermon. It often helps to take notes. Some of your notes will be simply informational ("The word 'leprosy' in NT times referred to many different skin diseases"); some will be to help remember important references ("Weeping may linger for the night, but joy comes with the morning." Ps. 30:5); some will be thoughts to reflect or act upon ("When was the last time you told your mother you love her?"); and some will be things you will be anxious to discuss later ("Of all Christians, Presbyterians are most like Pharisees."). Notes will never be a substitute for the experience of the sermon, or else God would have been satisfied to just give us God's own notes— the Bible. But notes can be ways of remembering the sermon, bringing it to life, savoring its benefits.

The Seventh Duty of Interpretation: Discuss the Sermon

Discuss the sermon. For some reason known only to God, many priests in the pew have the idea that when the minister stops speaking, the sermon is over. The opera doesn't end with the overture—it's only just begun. Through the sermon, God has introduced some themes into your mind and stirred your spirit in a particular way. God has prepared you for your priestly duty, and to imagine that your responsibilities are over as the sermon concludes is to call a halt to dinner preparations as soon as you've assembled the ingredients on the countertop.

It is precisely as the sermon approaches its resolution, in fact, that your true priestly duty emerges. The duties listed earlier in this chapter are intended to set the stage for what happens now—*your interpretation of the Word of God.* Your grappling with the themes or directions that have been opened to you in the sermon is what makes you an *interpreter* for the Lord, which is one of the three primary roles of a priest.

The Priest in the Pew as Interpreter. A fear that often surfaces when we Presbyterians admit to ourselves that we are each interpreters of the Word of God is that we have opened the door for everyone to interpret scripture to suit themselves. When everyone has the authority (indeed, the responsibility) to interpret scripture, who is to say that we will not turn astray like sheep, "everyone to his own way"?

And in point of fact, that danger exists. But we have always believed that the Spirit abides in the whole body of Christ, which is the priesthood of all believers. We trust God to lead this body in the path of righteousness, even if one or two of us are tempted to twist scripture to our own desires. For this reason, interpreters get together to compare what they have heard, and to test their interpretations against those in whom they trust.

For example, if your congregation has fellowship time after the service, you may have an opportunity to discuss what you've heard, thought, felt, and interpreted with fellow worshipers. Perhaps your pastor is willing to conduct (or simply observe) a lunchtime discussion. Try to involve all the leaders in the church. In general, the broader the discussion, and the more wise and mature Christians involved, the clearer God's voice becomes. Even if your discussion is only in the car on the way home, your understanding of God's word for you, your interpretation, becomes clearer and truer through mutual reflection. Such grappling with the Word of God in the sermon is an important part of every Christian's spiritual development.

I must also add that God has some peculiar habits in speaking to God's people. Most often, the body of Christ as a whole is properly tuned to God's word for the day. But God also sends prophets to the congregation, and in such cases the proper interpretation of God's words is a decidedly minority opinion. There is no hard and fast rule about who is correctly hearing the Word of God. While this fact teaches us humility, it in no way absolves us of our responsibility to interpret the Word expressed in scripture/sermon.

The Priest in the Pew as Translator. To prevent misunderstanding, we must also discuss the role of the priest as translator. No, this isn't about learning Hebrew or Greek. It's about *translating* your interpretation into action, and it is a natural extension of your active listening to the sermon. The preaching experience isn't over until the Spirit of Christ breathes within you, lifts you up, runs its course, and becomes part of your being. To use the analogy of a tree, if the mystery of God is the root of worship, if scripture is the trunk, if the pastor's sermon is a branch, if your discussion of the sermon is the twigs and leaves, then the change in the patterns and habits of your daily life is the blossom and fruit of Christ. At least occasionally, God will bring forth in you some insight, some decision, that significantly affects how you live. It need not even be a conscious experience on your part— maybe God stirs you subconsciously to bring forth a particular fruit of the Spirit in your life (love, joy, peace, patience, kindness, goodness, faithfulness, gentleness, self-control). This process of incorporating the Spirit, of the blossoming of Christ in your daily life, is the outgrowth of your tending to your worship responsibilities, and should take three or four days at least. If not, you need to listen to a sermon every forty-eight hours. (*That* prospect should be enough encouragement to fulfill this duty!)

Active listening involves carrying the Spirit out the door and into the world, *translating* the Word of God into visible dimensions of your daily life. You do well to demand relevance and application in a sermon. Often, however, the ball is dropped, not between scripture and sermon, but between pew and parking lot. The interpretation is there, but the translation is not. As you discuss the sermon and reflect on it, ask yourself, What can I do on

Wednesday to show God that I was working in the worship service on Sunday morning?

How to Listen to the Sermon

Let us return again to the metaphor of the revelation of God as a tree. If God is at the root of all reality, then scripture is the trunk through which God becomes known, and the sermon you are listening to on a given Sunday morning is a branch from that trunk. Your own reflection and action become the leaves and twigs, and occasionally, a blossom. What you are aiming for, in listening to the sermon, then, is to find a way to be grafted into the revelation of God in that particular moment.

This "grafting into the revelation of God" may be accomplished in any number of ways. You may choose to experience the sermon as:

1. A door. For example, "I am seeing an opportunity here to become involved in something I haven't done before" (a Bible study, Habitat for Humanity, college, letter-writing, tutoring, hospital visitation, political campaign, and so forth).
2. A window. Relax with the sermon. Open it wide and feel the love of God, the peace, the wisdom, the joy, the call of God blow through your soul.
3. A springboard. For instance, "While you were preaching, I thought about (the first time I saw snow; my aunt Margaret; the bike I haven't ridden in years). I remembered (some good I had done; to call my brother; a passage of scripture). I thanked God for (my mind; my parents; my country)."
4. A cattle prod. For example, "Ouch! I guess I've been carrying that grudge around far too long"; or " I really should have called my parents before now"; or "there's no reason to be quibbling over who will do the cleaning up."
5. God's delivery service. Somewhere in the sermon you will hear a verse of scripture that you will want to memorize and treasure; or a piece of information that looks just right on the wall of your mind; or a saying

that helps you remember to behave the way God would have you behave. Take the package joyfully and store it where it belongs.
6. God's lesson for the day. Write down and learn the main points of the sermon. File them within you. Then there's a chance you will remember them when they are useful.

You may notice that several of these ways of connecting with the sermon seem to involve something akin to daydreaming. This may not strike you as the kind of instruction that should be offered with respect to listening to a sermon. But if we are honest, we have to admit that daydreaming is something we all do at least occasionally when we're listening to a sermon. Do you think if you sit very still with your eyes facing front, God will not be able to tell if your mind is wandering? God knows our frailties, and still commands the Word to be preached. So you need to know that you can *guide* your daydreaming in such a way as to actually connect with God.

One thing you did not see in the list above is critiquing either the minister's style or the content of the sermon. Sometimes such critiquing is necessary and helpful. "Have you noticed, Reverend, that you cover your mouth near the end of many sentences? I often miss what you're trying to say when you do that." Or "you certainly know a lot about computers; but I sometimes get lost trying to see your point when your illustration involves Internet routing."

But as a general way of relating to a sermon, critiquing is not very useful. We are taught to critique all through our schooling, and in many places it is standard operating procedure—but not in church. The important issue of preaching, remember, is for you to be grafted into the revelation of God. Focusing on a peculiar habit or a repetitive phrase, though, can quite effectively *block* your connection to God. If your pastor can't seem to change when gently reminded and encouraged, then get over it. For some reason, God has chosen to speak to you in a way that requires more discipline than you had anticipated. Maybe your pastor reads the sermon, and that isn't as exciting for you. OK, well, maybe God is trying to *train your ear,* rather than *satisfy your eye.* Part of your service to God, then, is to make the adjustment and reconnect during the sermon. In a similar vein, don't focus on what doesn't make sense or apply to you. There are bound to be things the preacher says, if he or she is making any effort at all to relate scripture to daily life, that *don't* apply to your daily life this week. If you find something that isn't true for you this week, drop it and listen for something that does. (But be cautious—if you become agitated at how the sermon *most definitely does not* apply to you, give it some more thought when you get home.)

I do not mean to defend bad preaching. But bear in mind that God is able to reach anyone who is listening. Ask yourself whether you as a priest have shown yourself worthy of higher praise than that which you are bestowing on the preacher. If there is a lack of effort on the preacher's part, of course, someone should speak to him or her. The preacher has a vital task in the life of worship, and "Anyone unwilling to work should not eat" (2 Thess. 3:10). On the other hand, if the desire is there, and if training would help, the preacher should be allowed time and money for the training. In any event, you are connected spiritually with the person who is called to begin the interpretation process for your congregation, and all your interactions with him or her should reflect that spiritual reality.

REVIEW QUESTIONS

1. What is the most prominent feature of worship in our Presbyterian tradition?
2. List the seven priestly duties related to scripture and sermon in worship.
3. Why did the first Protestants think of scripture and sermon as a single element of worship?
4. Distinguish between an analytical and a faithful approach to scripture.
5. Using the metaphor of the tree, how is the mystery of God connected to your daily life by the scripture/sermon of worship?
6. What does it mean to speak of priestly listening as participation in a timely mystery? How does this explain why the preacher doesn't just get an old book of sermons and read one each Sunday? Or not show up to preach, but simply e-mail the sermon to all members?
7. Explain how you are an interpreter of scripture; a translator of scripture.

DISCUSSION QUESTIONS

1. Discuss the strengths of a sermon you have heard recently.
2. Can you think of a sermon through which, you are convinced, God spoke to you?
3. Which ways of listening to a sermon have you used?
4. Read scripture before the next worship service. Then gather and discuss whether anyone noticed a difference in the way God spoke to them during the sermon.
5. Pick a story from the Gospel of Luke, and write a short sermon.

Chapter 6

The Duties of the Priest: The Offering

What shall I return to the LORD for all his bounty to me? I will offer to you a thanksgiving sacrifice. . . . I will pay my vows to the LORD in the presence of all his people.
—Psalm 116:12, 17, 18

The Sacred Root

When worship as a mode of being fades from consciousness in the service, the loss is felt everywhere. Public prayers seem dry. Congregational singing fades to a whisper. The preaching struggles to avoid banality. But if one element of worship could be said to suffer the most from a lack of the religious presence of mind, the award would have to go to the offering.

One might think that the offering is so simple that it doesn't have anything to do with the religious presence of mind. What could be more straightforward and perfunctory than the act of offering? The plate comes by, you put your money in. In many Presbyterian worship services, a visitor could almost be excused for feeling that the offering is a break in the "religious action," an unpleasant but necessary pause for the gathering in of the money it takes to run the church.

This view of the offering has received impetus from the belief that money in general is unclean, "filthy lucre" (a phrase the King James Version of the Bible invokes to help translate various words meaning "greedy"). Thus money, the theory goes, should not be talked about in worship— even though Jesus teaches repeatedly about it; see, for example, Matthew 17:24–27; Mark 12:41–44; Luke 18:18–30. As long as these views and beliefs persist, as long as the priests in the pew are ignorant of the sacred root of the offering, the worship service will always have a hole in it for the collection of the offering.

Actually the act of offering is easily on a plane with the most sacred and holy acts we perform as priests. Putting money in the offering is as significant as taking bread from the Communion plate. Only a pall of ignorance, settling on the priesthood assembled in the pews, could account for our lack of awareness of the holiness of our offering. In order to understand our priestly duties in this area of worship, we must reacquaint ourselves with the sacred root of the offering: stewardship.

True Stewardship

One of the contributing factors to the significance of the offering is obvious to even the unbeliever: the value of money. Our money is very precious to us. We worked hard to get it, and it provides many of the things we need and want. So to give it up freely, even to God, is an act of either insanity or love. By the same token, our offering is very precious to the church. Local Presbyterian churches rely almost exclusively for their very existence on the money put into the offering plate. No member wants to see *any* church close its doors, and the Presbyterian expression of Christianity would face almost certain extinction if *all* our churches closed their doors. Yet that fate is averted only by the offerings that worshipers make.

But the sacredness of the offering has still more profound roots than the value of the money itself. The offering is rooted in, and grows from, God. We are children of God, we spring from God's love. Ultimately we will return to God. In between, there is no part of our life that is not God's. The fact that Jesus is "the Alpha and the Omega, the beginning and the end" (Rev. 21:6), the fact that it is God in whom "we live and move and have our being" (Acts 17:28), and the fact that my "only comfort, in life and in death . . . [is] that I belong—body and soul, in life and in death—not to myself, but to my faithful Savior, Jesus Christ"[1] create in the fiber of our being a relationship to God that we call stewardship.

As Christians we belong to God; we are God's servants. "It is [God] that made us, and we are his" (Ps. 100:3). No Christian *owns* any money—not a single penny. Each Christian is assigned the duty, and granted the privilege, of managing a *life,* including a certain amount of money, that belongs to our Superior. That life is a portion (however small) of God's wealth; each Christian has thus been created to be a manager (or *steward*) of a little bit of God's astounding creation. That is why we call the Christian management of *all* money *steward*ship.

When we realize that we as priests are handling *God's* money, many new and profound questions arise, among which are:

1. What luxuries does God intend through the moneys entrusted to me?
2. Is God's house as well cared for as the homes of God's stewards, or are the servants living higher than the master?
3. Do my daily priorities serve the interests of my Superior?
4. Whom do I trust as an investment counselor with God's wealth?
5. What is my role with respect to my fellow stewards (that is, church members)? What is my responsibility to encourage them to be accountable also?
6. Can I see God's will in my MasterCard bill? My checking account statement? The church's annual budget?

These are the kinds of questions a priest must ask. Without these questions, faith and treasure go their separate ways, and we end up trying to do the impossible—serve two masters. Gone is worship as a mode of being from the weekly offering, and with it any hope for the religious presence of mind. Gone also is the Holy Spirit from every financial transaction. "No one can serve two masters; for either he will hate the one and love the other, or he will be devoted to the one and despise the other. You cannot serve God and mammon" (Matt. 6:24 RSV).

God knows our needs and provides for us. Yet we are so quickly swept up in anxiety or greed, and find ourselves secretly in service to mammon. The failure to tithe, the hiding of the lesser god in bank accounts and mutual funds, worshiping it with payment books and credit cards—this is what is holding the church spiritually hostage in the world today.

When we tithe every Sunday, we kill this false god; we sacrifice mammon and lay its heart at our Redeemer's feet. Nothing could indicate more clearly that mammon is no god at all, that money has no hold on us, than to take our money and offer it freely to God. This victory over mammon is far more than a matter of money—it is a triumph over "the spiritual forces of evil in the heavenly places" (Eph. 6:12), which threaten continually to take hold of our hearts and our lives.

Stewardship and God's Love

There is a lesson for us in the story of the rich young man who comes to Jesus wanting to inherit eternal life (Mark 10:17–22). Jesus reminds him of the commandments (a lesson in itself), and when the young man replies, "Teacher, I have kept all these [commandments] since my youth," Mark reports the following:

> Jesus, looking at him, loved him and said, "You lack one thing; go, sell what you own, and give the money to the poor, and you will have treasure in heaven; then come, follow me" (10:21).

Why Jesus commanded the young man to divest himself remains uncertain. But if we believe in Christ, we believe that Jesus' instructions reflect both divine wisdom and divine *love*. Jesus did not intend to punish the young man, but to set him free. It may be that Jesus recognized that the young man's happiness depended upon actually being a disciple, just like Peter and the others. Since possessions require much time and energy, however, the only way this hungering seeker could become a full-time disciple would be to let go of his possessions, free himself totally from those "golden handcuffs," and give himself over to his call. But the young man could not do this, and so he returned to his own wealthy misery. He had fallen in love with the god with whom he had spent his time, for whom he had offered his energy, from whom he had obtained his station in life, in whom he had placed his hope, to whom he had sworn allegiance. So he went away from the Truth, miserable, when he could have embraced it and ambled into joy.

I would guess that the lure of financial security, financial success, financial freedom has kept many a person from his or her call. How many doors would we be opening if as a church people we altered our priorities and worshiped the one true God, instead of secretly worshiping money? We could create a community and an environment in which it seems only natural to shed the golden handcuffs. How many more musicians and dancers, artisans and saints, healers and prophets would we be sending out into the world to transform it, if only we understood and practiced stewardship? What would be the effect felt in doctors' offices and government offices, in boardrooms and courtrooms, if every Christian sacrificed mammon to God every Sunday?

My Money, My Self

You may believe that there is no god called mammon, that to claim its existence is merely a projection of our own selfish nature into the world beyond, and a deification of the image we have come up with. Perhaps you are right—perhaps there is no spirit of mammon in the universe. But if mammon does not exist *ex*ternal to us, if the evil and slavery associated with money is *in*ternal to us, we are forced to admit that it is part of our *selves* which we are sacrificing when we put our money in the offering plate.

There is poverty in America; there is financial hardship. But surely there is also great blessing and financial abundance. Something other than financial hardship is holding many people back from tithing to God. For many of us, it isn't that we don't have money, it's that we don't want to part with it. We love money. And whether we feel comfortable or not in admitting it, our love of money (just as our love of anyone or anything) is a very personal thing, a part of our selves. Thus to give up something we love to God is to give God a part of our selves. It is our very selves that we are sacrificing when we place our offering in the plate on Sunday morning.

While this conclusion seems to accord nicely with Paul's instructions to "present [our] bodies as a living sacrifice, holy

and acceptable to God, which is [our] spiritual worship" (Rom.
12:1), it does raise two related questions: (1) How does *money*
become so much a part of us that offering money is equivalent to
offering our *bodies*? and (2) How can *money* be holy and acceptable to God?

Our Money Is Us

I begin with the assertion that our money *is* us. It is what we have
to show for the week(s) we have worked to receive it. For most
of us, the majority of all the personal resources available to us
during the work week—our time, thought, energy, sweat—went
into the earning of the money that we received on payday. We
paid a very high price for our wages—we gave our *selves* to our
work. And for many of us, the one tangible dividend for all this
time employed at work is the money we now have at our disposal.
The effect of working, then, is to convert a significant amount of
our spiritual *being* (by *being* I mean our *livingness*—our breath,
thoughts, speech, actions, ideas, discipline, memory, analytical
gifts, personal awareness and sensitivity, and so forth—precisely
what Paul meant by the word *bodies*) into money. What we *were*
remains present in two ways: in the intangible effect we had on
the world, and in the tangible presence of monetary income. As
we look at our paycheck, we are looking at our self, our being,
our body, distilled into economic power.

Our money is not only who we have been, but also *who we will
be*. Everything our money will be converted into—shelter, suste-
nance, education, entertainment—is a true expression of our
bodies, our selves. *You* will select a house or apartment or con-
dominium or mobile home for your self; *you,* and no one else,
will furnish it in ways that express you most personally. Your car,
your clothes, the movies you choose to see, the golf clubs you
acquire to improve your game—all these things are expressions
of you, and taken together they give a pretty good picture of you.
They certainly all contribute mightily to the way the world per-
ceives you.

When we want to convince a friend that he or she looks good
in a particular jacket, we may say, "It's *you*." And if our friend

has the same sense about it, and buys the jacket, then it actually *becomes* (at least one part or dimension of) him or her. So one might say that a particular dimension of our friend *emerged* from the money of his or her income. Until the person actually bought the jacket, that expression of him or her was merely potential. Without the money, however, there would have been no potential. So when we look at our money, we are looking at a significant portion of the potential we have to express and present ourselves to the world. We are looking at who we will be.

A large part of me that is past is presently distilled into money. A large part of me that is potential for the future is currently inherent in money. In ways more profound than we may be willing to admit, our money is us. Our bodies' past and future are (temporarily, at any rate) stored as money. When we put *that* money into the offering plate, we present our bodies as a living sacrifice.

Our Money Is Holy

Since we are priests, holy to God, and our money is a distillation of our selves, our money is also holy. At first blush, this might sound strange, but since God has sanctified us "not in part, but the whole," *our money is holy.* Not *all* money is holy. (Scripture teaches us that the love of money is the root of all evil [1 Tim. 6:10], and how could the love of something holy be the root of evil?) But *our* money is holy because *we* are holy. God has called us out of darkness into God's marvelous light. Since our money is the distillation of our selves, our money has also been called out of the same darkness, into the same light.

When God made a claim on me, the claim was not partial. Nor did God sift through my years or my experiences, sanctifying some and ignoring others. I believe I have been clothed entirely in the righteousness of Jesus Christ. If God has sanctified me entirely, then God has sanctified my money. If I, as a child of God, am holy, then my money is holy, just as my body is holy, my imagination is holy, my life's goals are holy. Every time I write a check, I am disbursing something holy, something very much a part of my body, my self. When I pay the utilities, buy groceries, subscribe to the paper, make a mortgage payment or contribute to the church, I am doing the work of a priest, because I am handling something holy.

Because the doctrine of the priesthood of all believers has fallen into desuetude, we easily lose sight of the fact that our first career and calling in life is to serve the living God. In the typical Presbyterian worship service, much is made of what we have been saved *from*; worship is what we have been saved *to*. To live is to worship; to worship is to live—and not just during the formally appointed hour for worship. We have been saved for and to much more than an hour a week. The purpose and blessing of our salvation is to wait upon God completely and continually. Our salvation is so complete that our holiness permeates our checkbooks; our service is so complete that it governs our saving and spending.

Herein lies the spiritual significance of the offering and the door to the religious presence of mind. With the act of offering every Sunday morning, we acknowledge our continuing temptation to serve mammon, and at the same time we celebrate the victory—and the Life that flows from the victory—by presenting our bodies as a living sacrifice to the one true God. The love of money is the greatest threat to our spiritual well-being; the act of offering protects us from this bondage. "For freedom Christ has set us free. Stand firm, therefore, and do not submit again to a yoke of slavery" (Gal. 5:1).

Stewardship and the Local Church

In this day and age, we are constantly besieged by folks wanting our money for various causes; some of them natural and understandable; some of them noble; some of them reprehensible. People on TV shout at us to buy their cars; they call us on the phone at suppertime to sell us year-round pest control; they send us bulk-mail appeals for help in defending the environment; they knock on our doors to sell us band candy.

And at least once a year, most Presbyterian churches have a "stewardship campaign," in which members are encouraged to make a pledge for the coming year. In our consumeristic, money-hungry society, it is only natural that the church's talk about stewardship should seem to be just one more demand in the staggering number of appeals for our money. This idea is perpetuated by many stewardship campaigns, which focus on how much "bang for the buck" the member receives, in terms of program, mission, staff, and building.

Perhaps you will notice a disparity between the meaning of the offering and the focus of the pledge drive, which many of our denominations and churches conduct in the fall of the year. The duty of the priest is to handle his or her income in a manner worthy of its holiness. A part of any such handling is the presentation of an offering to God. Yet so many so-called stewardship campaigns seem to focus almost exclusively on the needs of the local church. If the offering is primarily an act of love between the believer and God, why is there so much emphasis on making sure there's enough money to pay the church's bills?

At the heart of this problem is a misconception about the offering. For many Presbyterians, there is an unspoken belief that the point of giving to the church is to support the church and its activities. What one pledges to the church, then, is dependent upon the church's needs. If the church cannot demonstrate a need for increased giving, there is no point in giving any more. It is as if God says to us, "My only financial concern is the survival of the church; if you've contributed in some way to that, you are free to spend the rest of your income any way you like."

One does not give *to* the church; one gives *through* the church to God. What passes *through* the church performs the vital task of sustaining and growing the community of believers. In a wealthy country like our own, there is an abundance left over with which to minister to the larger world. In fact, where stewardship is strong, the governing board of the church is faced with how to faithfully handle the surplus, not how to whittle the church's needs down to meet the giving.

The advertising world has been successful in large part due to its ability to convince us that falling behind the Joneses is a major tragedy; not having the right athletic shoes, a late model car, the most current options on our TV, or a new home is somehow demeaning, embarrassing, even debilitating. So what is originally intended for God is diverted to material purposes, as we attempt to live at, or beyond, the threshold of financial capability. It falls to the church, then, to suffer what each of us secretly fears—to be demeaned, to be embarrassed, to be debilitated.

True stewardship restores spiritual strength to the believer, credibility to the priest, ability and influence to the church, and honor to God. Only good can come from it. "Whoever would save his life will lose it; and whoever loses his life for my sake and the gospel's will save it" (Matt. 10:39). It's true.

Fiscal Responsibility

Stewardship does not end when we drop our envelope in the plate. There is also the matter of stewardship of the *church's* finances. We—you and I—have a responsibility, first of all, to see that all moneys are handled by a capable and reliable person, according to generally accepted accounting practices.

Beyond this basic principle, we also have the responsibility of seeing that church moneys are directed toward the kingdom of God. Surely a certain percentage of the church budget should be spent on ministries of compassion—locally, nationally, and/or around the world. The Christian education program should not have to make do with outdated materials and constantly shrinking supplies. The children of the church are *our* children—all of them. We have promised to nurture them with both our attention and our wallet. As far as the building and grounds are concerned, I may say with the confidence that comes from experience that no one saves money in the long run by going with cheaper materials when repairing the House of God. The church will be around long after we have gone, and it will bear silent witness to the quality we have put into it. We are simply passing on a larger bill to our descendants by taking shortcuts in the maintenance and repair of the church. The first three principles to keep in mind when maintaining, repairing, or renovating the church are (1) quality; (2) quality; and (3) quality.

Duties

Once the congregation has the proper understanding of stewardship, the actual duties of the offering are quite simple. They are threefold: preparation, presentation, and promise.

The First Duty of the Offering: Preparation

Proper preparation for the offering begins with a consideration of our financial condition. What is my income? What is God giving me to manage and live on? What are my financial responsibilities? This book is not primarily about the subject of stewardship, but a word should be said here about the major financial commitments in life. A wise and just steward does not commit himself or herself to large car payments and large mortgage payments, and then complain to God that there's just no money available for the offering. The time to consider our stewardship is *before* we decide on a car or a house. If we live within our means, we'll have money for God, not to mention more options with what is left for ourselves.

A simple, practical dimension to preparing your offering is to follow the guidelines of your financial officers. If your church's custom is to distribute pledge envelopes for you to use in making your offering, *please use them* and place whatever information is requested on the outside of the envelope. This is a courtesy to the persons keeping track of the contributions, who in most churches are volunteers. A small effort on your part will greatly lighten their load, and after all, they are your fellow priests.

The Second Duty of the Offering: Presentation

The actual presentation of the offering (which includes placing the envelope in the offering plate and whatever presentation is then done with the offering plates themselves) is almost a sacrament. The offering is similar to adult baptism in that it represents us submitting and offering ourselves as living sacrifices to God. It is also similar to Communion in that we share with God what is most precious to us, our very selves, as Jesus shared his precious body and blood. Like the ancient sacrifices of the Old Testament, the Worshiped and the worshiper share the bounty that God has supplied, enjoying fellowship with each other in the beauty of the sanctuary.

Given the sanctity of the offering, I am of the opinion that the proper way to begin is with a confession of sin. Some of our churches avoid public confession altogether, but I cannot bring myself to believe that I am a worthy offering apart from the immediate grace and forgiveness of God. I find that confession serves to clear the air. Confession teaches us humility by awakening in us an awareness of our dependence on God's grace. The assurance of forgiveness (or declaration of pardon) comforts us with the knowledge that our righteousness is a gift from Christ, not the result of our behavior the previous week or the amount of our check. If we are to present our selves as a living sacrifice, *holy* and *acceptable to God,* we will want to be clean as only God can make us. So if your church's custom does include public confession of sin, certainly *one* appropriate place for a prayer of confession would be as an introduction to the offering.

In many churches, the offering itself consists of the ushers passing the offering plates down the rows of pews. The plates are then brought to the front (where there may be a prayer of dedication) or carried to the back.

Within this process there are two important moments for each worshiper. The first is the moment when you place your envelope in the offering plate. This is the *individual* moment of offering, the act in which you re-offer yourself to God. The individual moment of offering is the appropriate time for a simple prayer like, "Here I am, Lord." The chances are slight that anything you do in the coming week will be as dramatic in terms of giving yourself to God as the act of placing your offering in the plate. This is the moment of trust, obedience, sacrifice, and true, agape love.

For this reason, there is something to be said for putting in a check *each* Sunday service. I realize that it is more convenient to pay a pledge once a month (for some, even once a year). And one may rightly point out that more is spent on checks, envelopes, and so forth if a check is written every week. A check every week also increases the workload of the folks who count the money.

As much as my sympathies are with the hard-working, faithful volunteers who count the offering, though, the offering is vital to worship. After all, it would be more economical to *worship* once a year and save air-conditioning or heating, but "is not life more than food, and the body more than clothing?" (Matt. 6:25). Of course it is! Life is *worship,* and our spiritual worship, as Paul says, is the presentation of our selves as a living sacrifice. Writing a check every Sunday may not be efficient, but there are matters more important than efficiency (if I may be so blasphemous as to suggest that thought in a culture which regards business as normative for all life). We as a culture are in danger of economizing ourselves right out of being human. Whatever expense is incurred, in terms of time or money, by the necessities of worship, is simply part of the cost of being human. With training and experience, the priest comes to value every individual moment of offering.

Lastly, if the offering plates are brought forward at the conclusion of the ingathering, the ushers should be informed that they are bringing the *lives* of the members before the throne of God. Their behavior and handling of the plates should reflect the sanctity of the offering.

At the point at which the ushers are bringing the offering forward, though, only one presentation has been made: the individual presentation that each member placed in the plate as it passed down the row. If our own personal offering were all that God sought, we could end the offering at this point—in fact we could mail it in, and never come to church to offer anything.

But we are not simply an assortment of individuals. We are the church, the (one, united) body of Christ, so it is only natural that the final act of presentation be a corporate act, the act of the whole church together. It is appropriate, as the corporate presentation begins, to stand as a church body and sing praise to the God who has so richly blessed us as a people. As the ushers bring the lives of the members forward to the cross and Communion table, they lay the offering of the whole church (its members, its money) before God. Just as the *individual* moment of offering is an opportunity for prayer (for example, "Here I am, Lord"), so is the *corporate* moment of offering. Such a prayer of dedication may be as follows:

> "Here we *all* are, Lord. We thank and praise you for having washed this congregation in the blood of Jesus and having sanctified us in this hour. We present this offering to you as earnest money, a sign of the earnest commitment of our lives in the coming week. The offering is yours; we are yours.

Govern our gifts, hearts, hands, and lips individually and as a church body, we ask in Jesus' name, Amen.

The Third Duty of the Offering: Promise

I noted above that our money is in one sense the potential expression of us, that is, the as yet unselected future. So when we put our money into the offering plate, when we lay it before the throne of God, we are turning over a part of our future to God, letting God decide how the money we have offered will become an expression of us in the next week, month, or year. Maybe the part of us we put in the offering plate will be turned into coal to heat the building, or into crayons for the kindergarten class. Maybe it will be given directly to the pastor to help support the family, or directly to the bank to keep the doors of the church open. Whatever its purpose, we have laid part of our own future at God's throne.

And since for most of us, it's the part we most struggle to part with, what better time than the offering to promise God the *rest* of our future as well? Our offering to God is not simply an expression of gratitude for what God has done for us in the past, it is a promise on our part, a down payment or first installment on the bill of our future. We owe everything to God, and the offering is the first major demonstration that we intend to keep the bargain. There's a familiar hymn that goes, "Take my life and let it be consecrated, Lord, to thee." The hymn itself is an offering and a promise, and it carries a lot more weight when we have demonstrated our commitment with the money that is so precious to us.

It is the promise made in the offering, more than any stirring words of the sermon or any uplift from the music, that serves as the bridge over which worship as a mode of being passes from the sanctuary into the home and workplace. If the offering is not sacrificial, the foundation of the bridge is small. The bridge itself must therefore be small, and will hold little traffic. The chasm between worship and weekday life remains. If the offering is sacrificial, the foundation of the bridge is massive, and every aspect of our lives begins to feel the impact of worship as a mode of being.

You will note the element of promise in the prayer of dedication printed above. Even a personal, silent prayer like "here is my money, Lord, and with it my heart and soul; take my life in this coming week and do with it as you will" will cover the duty of promise inherent in the offering. But an offering is not really complete without some expression of commitment for the future.

Conclusion

To summarize our duties with respect to the offering, then, we have a duty to (1) *prepare* a worthy offering; (2) *present* ourselves humbly with prayer; and (3) *promise* the fulfillment of our obedience in the coming week.

REVIEW QUESTIONS

1. List the three duties of the offering.
2. What is the sacred root of the offering?
3. What does *steward* mean?
4. What was Jesus' attitude toward the rich young man?
5. Explain how "our money is us."
6. Why is our money holy?
7. What advantage is there to making an offering every Sunday?

DISCUSSION QUESTIONS

1. Have you ever experienced the religious presence of mind during the Sunday morning offering? Why or why not?
2. Which gets more attention in your congregation during stewardship season: true stewardship or the church's financial needs?
3. Put together a prayer of dedication for the whole church's offering.
4. In what ways can a person carry the sacred root of the offering to the other six days of the week?
5. How is your church using your self (that is, your offering) to glorify God?

Chapter 7

The Duties of the Priest: Communion

"This is my body, which is given for you."

—Luke 22:19

*O*n October 4, 1998, at four o'clock in the afternoon at the University of Chicago's Rockefeller Chapel, a remarkable event took place. Four mainline Protestant traditions—the Evangelical Lutheran Church in America, the Presbyterian Church (U.S.A.), the Reformed Church in America, and the United Church of Christ—came together for the Lord's Supper. The culmination of thirty-five years of formal theological dialogue (study, reflection, sharing, and listening), this Communion service was a visible manifestation of the full communion that all four traditions have joined together to create.

Not least of the miraculous dimensions of this event is that it took us more than 400 years to achieve. At the Colloquy of Marburg, in 1529, it became apparent to the early leaders of the Protestant Reformation that, despite many areas of agreement among Protestants, there was something about Communion that would make it difficult for the various branches of the movement to come together.

There were fifteen points of discussion at Marburg; the Reformers agreed on fourteen. Regarding the last, they wrote: ". . . we have not reached agreement as to whether the true body and blood of Christ are in the bread and wine bodily."[1]

Perhaps one reason the Reformers could not come together on the subject of Communion was because the sacrament is so vital to Christian worship and life. The Lord's Supper is one of the great wellsprings of faith, a reliable source of the religious presence of mind, absolutely essential to our walk with God. It is difficult to compromise in an area that means so much to so many. What might be lost from the root of my faith if I let go of the profound insight of my own tradition?

Yet even the Reformers' lack of agreement can teach us something. The first lesson to be learned from the painstakingly slow efforts to achieve consensus on Communion is how vast, and ultimately how inexpressible, is the mystery of the Lord's Supper. Each of our traditions testifies to some dimension(s) of the sacrament; none of our traditions incorporates them all.

Even within our own Presbyterian tradition, there is probably a fair amount of latitude in the understandings among the priests in the pews, the folks who gather regularly for worship. John Calvin expressed the belief that in the moment of sharing the Lord's Supper, the whole congregation is lifted up to heaven to be with Christ;[2] but I wonder, if we were to take an exit poll following a Communion service at one of our churches, whether Calvin's belief would rank as the most frequently mentioned interpretation of the worshipers' experience of the just completed Lord's Supper.

Not that it would need to; not that Calvin's way is *the* right or only way to view Communion. As Presbyterians, we should be aware of Calvin's understanding, but as unique, faithful Christians, we are not bound by any one interpretation. I hope in the following paragraphs to stimulate your thought and intuition on the mystery of Communion, and more than that, to clarify some of the duties incumbent upon us as priests, which are set forth by God precisely to open a door into the world of grace and power, which is the sacrament of the Lord's Supper.

Cognitive Knowledge of Communion

Let's start with our strength as Presbyterians—the *cognitive* knowledge of Communion. By *cognitive* I mean, essentially, the knowledge that is expressed in *words,* whether thought, spoken, or written. It is knowledge we can articulate, record, share through impersonal means like books. To some of us, it might seem like cognitive is the *only* kind of knowledge; but there are other ways of knowing.

We Presbyterians have always placed great emphasis on cognitive knowledge generally, and on the cognitive dimension of Communion in particular. We're good at analyzing and developing lines of thought. It's one of the great contributions we make to the larger Christian tradition. Theology is primarily cognitive, and the Reformed tradition contains much theology about Communion.

So much has been written about Communion, in fact, that I have little new to offer in the way of cognitive knowledge of the sacrament. Your pastor will be able to direct you to some of the rich and inspiring literature. Before proceeding to the discussion of other ways of knowing Communion, though, let me simply offer three directions that you may find helpful as you grow in your cognitive knowledge of the sacrament.

They are as follows: First, while we have always placed great emphasis on the *elements* of Communion, we also benefit from devoting attention to the *actions* of Communion. Second, without discrediting the *personal* nature of Communion, we enrich our worship life by examining its *corporate* nature as well. Finally, even as we maintain our tradition of *unadorned* Communion, we must guard against it slipping into *casual* Communion.

The Actions of Communion

Protestants in general have argued over Christ's presence in the elements of Communion for hundreds of years. We Presbyterians debate among ourselves. The odds of resolving the question seem quite small, actually. I will only say that as I see it, with regard to the bread and wine, *no* physical changes occur, *and* the elements are still the body and blood of Christ. Communion is something that must be believed to be understood, not vice versa. And try as I might, I cannot imagine Jesus being anxious over this question. He made no effort to explain it to his disciples (Mark 14:22ff.), though he explained many things to them privately (see Mark 4:34).

The elements are merely the material basis for Christ's spirit, just as our bodies are the material basis of our spirit. Matter and spirit are intimately connected; no human spirit acts without a body. But to focus only on the *matter* is to pretend that the spirit doesn't even exist, that the sacrament has somehow died. To pick at the bread and wine, trying to find Christ, is to conduct an autopsy on Communion.

We ought rather to ask, how is the *spirit* present? What *actions,* what *movements* are taking place? There are three sources of activity/action/movement. The first source of action is Jesus, on the night of his arrest, suddenly redirecting the flow of faith in the Seder (the meal that begins Passover) by declaring, in what we call now the act of institution, that the bread is his body; the wine, his blood. The second source is the movement of the bread and wine—broken and poured out, distributed and nourishing. The third source or locus of activity is the equally important action of the disciples, raising the bread to their lips, drinking the wine of their own free will. In these actions, the Spirit of Christ makes itself apparent to believers.

To appreciate how important the *movement* of Communion is, compare the sacrament to a musical concert. When you attend a concert, where is the music? There is no music on the score—only ink is on the score. There is no music in the instruments—the instruments could sit on stage all night and not produce a sound. The music is not even in the musicians—if it were only in the musicians, it couldn't be heard.

The music is in the performance, the actions, the movement of the spirit, the expressed passion. When the performance ends, the music ends. The score, the instruments, the musicians—all these continue to exist, but the music is gone.

Communion is Christ's concert. Jesus is present in the elements-and-actions, the whole experience of sharing the bread and wine. When the *act* of Communion is past, so too passes that sacramental awareness of Christ's Spirit. Another way of saying the same thing is to say that Jesus is not present *because of* our eating and drinking; he is present *in* our eating and drinking.

Corporate Communion

Paul wrote to the Corinthians that "all who eat and drink without discerning the body, eat and drink judgment against themselves"

(1 Cor. 11:29). The "body" that Paul is talking about is not the bread representing the body of Christ, as if someone might be taking Communion without knowing that the bread was Christ's body. The "body" in this verse is the *church.*

The "body" is one of Paul's favorite ways of talking about the church. He writes in the same letter to the Corinthians, "For in the one Spirit we were all baptized into one body . . ." (12:13) and again, ". . . *you* [pl.] are the body of Christ and individually members of it" (12:27). Indeed, according to Paul, God has composed the body, that is, the church, in its particular way, for one purpose: "that there may be no dissension within the body, but the members may have the same care for one another" (12:25). Paul is upset with the Corinthians because the body, which is the church, suffers when "each of you goes ahead with your own supper, and one goes hungry and another becomes drunk. . . . [D]o you show contempt for the church of God and humiliate those who have nothing?" (11:21, 22). "[W]hen you come together to eat, *wait for one another*" (11:33; emphasis mine).

Such language about eating and drinking judgment on oneself might seem a bit strong if the issue of waiting for one another were simply a matter of manners. But "discerning the body," recognizing that it is a whole *church* which is taking Communion, is a far deeper issue than mere courtesy or etiquette.

Jesus never served Communion to one disciple alone. Part of the mystery of Communion is that it creates the body of Christ, as everyone in the church moves at the command, and in the spirit, of the church's head, Jesus. It is the body of the church that is nourished by Christ. We are more than a cluster of individuals (as would be the case, for instance, of a crowd in the dining room at a McDonald's). We are some kind of organic, spiritual comm*unity.*

Thus it is the church that, though very much enmeshed in the flesh, with all its desires and defenses, its interpersonal struggles and uneven commitment, becomes more and more like Christ as it feeds on him. It is the *church* body that receives Communion, it is the *church* body that is nourished and grows. Each individual member benefits from Communion primarily through the whole body, the church, and only secondarily as a personal worshiper. So while your own personal experience of Communion is not to be in any way downplayed, Communion is primarily for the benefit of the *whole* church, and secondarily, for your benefit as well, since you are a member of the church.

As each of us changes individually during our lifetime, so does the church. Feeding on the proper food, it upbuilds itself in love, actually acquiring a different feel, a different atmosphere as the reality of Christ's Spirit takes hold. I do not deny in any way that a church has faults. After all, it is made up of human beings. But the church that feeds on Christ is a rare and special thing among all the various groups that we human beings comprise. It is the body of the church that we must discern when we take Communion.

This discerning of the body is especially important when we are in a spiritual trough, or worse, the dark night of the soul. When we find our souls empty of faith, we may take comfort in the fact that the body is still receiving Christ; and as part of the body, so are we. We are like waves on a lake, reflecting the brightness of the sun. When we are high, full of faith, we reflect God's glory. When we are not, we simply provide a backdrop for those around us who are. One little wave bouncing up and down by itself may experience the discomfort of a spiritual roller coaster, and not reflect much of God's glory. But as part of a whole lake—the whole church—we contribute to a spectacular sight in God's eyes. It is not too much to say that faith rests in the body of the church, more than in any one individual, since all of us experience doubts at some time or other.

"Unadorned" vs. "Casual" Communion

In our effort to strip Christianity of magical connotations and unnecessary pomp, we Presbyterians have tended to overlook the setting of the first Lord's Supper. Jesus did institute a sacrament elegant in its simplicity, but he chose the Seder, the Passover meal, as the setting from which his revelation was to emerge. For all Jews, this was and is a time of ancient custom and profound ritual. As they sat around the table that evening, the disciples were participating in a religious rite whose meaning had been refined and deepened by a thousand years of practice. Through the recitation of prayers and scripture, the singing of songs, the sharing of sacred food, the recollection of their roots, and the spiritual joining with their ancestors in *their* experience of God, the disciples were keenly attuned to God's presence. The bread was *already* holy to them, the wine was *already* sacred, before Jesus had done anything. Every corner of their souls was stirred by the words and actions of the ceremony. This was the hour they most trusted God, the hour of their most intense experience of the religious presence of mind.

Only within this sacred time did Jesus institute the Lord's Supper. The lengthy and careful preparation for Passover had served to "rope off" the revelation. The disciples were aware of being on holy ground. They were in the midst of worship when Jesus revealed God afresh to them. This was no mere cognitive experience, no simple passing on of information. The whole night spoke to them on all levels of knowing.

Unfortunately, too many of our churches seem to make no special preparation for Communion whatsoever. In a typical Presbyterian church, in which Communion is celebrated monthly or quarterly, I would guess that more than half the worshipers are surprised to learn, upon arrival at church, that Communion is taking place that day. There has been no preparation prior to the service itself on the part of those who are not specifically charged with preparing the elements.

Nor is much done in the service itself prior to the sacrament to allow the priests in the pews to properly prepare themselves. The Communion that results from this preparation may well be unadorned and simple, but it is also far too casual and mechanical. I wholeheartedly agree with the traditional Protestant opposition to the kind of pomp surrounding Communion, which changes the sacrament into something it was never intended to be; but a travesty of equal magnitude is committed by confusing "unadorned" with "casual." Keep it simple, yes; but also, keep it sacred. Rope off Communion with scripture, music, prayer, and meditation. Otherwise "unadorned" is no virtue at all, but a euphemism for *casual.*

Beyond the Cognitive:
Other Ways of Knowing Communion

The beauty and power of a sacrament is that God's presence, word, will, and grace are communicated to us on *all* the levels of human knowing. Though we will have to admit at some point that God is beyond all human knowledge, we need not limit ourselves even further by confining ourselves to what we can *think* (or say or write) about God. There is awareness without words; there is understanding beyond articulation; there is wisdom deeper than reason. We recognize the inspiration of Jesus in establishing a sacred act that is not limited, in its meaning or power, to what we can express verbally.

Our greatest danger as Presbyterians is to harbor the unspoken belief that actually everything about Communion can be put into words, that the sacrament is rationally understandable. Such a belief constricts our access to God terribly, but it is in our nature to believe so. Before we look at other ways of knowing God, then, let us satisfy ourselves that Communion is both too broad and too deep to be grasped cognitively.

First of all, Communion is too *broad* to be grasped cognitively because it covers too much ground. There is simply too much cognitive information about Communion for the whole of it to be held simultaneously in the consciousness. When we start to gather all the information in our minds, the first data fall out before the last are taken in. Can we consider the whole life of Jesus, his miracles, his sermons, his crucifixion and resurrection (in fulfillment of the command to "do this in remembrance of me" [Luke 22:19])? Can we add to that the meaning of the symbolism of the bread and juice (including their role in the Seder meal); the life situations of the people we are worshiping with; the interpretation of the sacrament that the preacher has recently put forth; the direction in which the church is headed; the teachings of our tradition; and our own thoughts on Communion—all this at the same time as we eat the bread and drink the juice?

Everything ever written on Communion still has not exhausted the dimensions of Communion about which it is possible to talk and write. No one could be aware of all of it, much less all at once in the moment of worship.

And Communion is also too deep for our cognitive minds, because the sacrament is first of all an *experience,* not a concept or a doctrine. Experiential knowledge doesn't end at the boundary of words. Experience teaches us in many nonverbal ways, among which might be listed the *sensory,* the *visceral,* and the *intuitive.*

In the printed medium, I can talk *about* these other ways of knowing, but I can't create them. To discuss them is to convert them, by definition, into *cognitive* knowledge, and something (I might argue, *everything*) is lost in the translation. Can I capture in an essay the power of Beethoven's *Missa Solemnis?* Will a newspaper article do justice to the experience of piloting an airplane? Will words ever convey exactly how you used to feel in your grandmother's kitchen? In each of these experiences, something of the real world is absorbed by those involved; knowledge that is acquired cannot be precisely conveyed via the cognitive dimension.

The same is true of Communion. How can we discuss the level of *sensory* knowledge, for instance? What good would it do to try to put into words the way the bread feels in your hand, or the way the glass feels as you bring it to your lips? The sound of the trays moving along the pews; the sight of the congregation in devotion; the native aroma of your sanctuary—through all these sensory experiences one comes to know God in the Lord's Supper.

There is also the *visceral* knowledge of the tradition in which we are immersed as we take Communion. Just as the disciples were steeped in the visceral knowledge of the Seder and Passover, we are now integrally woven into the tradition of Christian Communion. For 2,000 years, men and women have been gathering at the Table, hearing the words of institution, feeding on the body and blood of Jesus. The invitation has been uttered in hundreds of languages, and accepted by millions of people. In abundance and in want, in persecution and in triumphalism, in grief, in hope, and in just plain living, the Spirit of Jesus has risen to awareness again and again in the sharing of the bread and the wine.

Those born into the Christian tradition who attempt to find

their own way *apart* from the Christian faith are undertaking a far greater transformation than what Jesus pursued. They are cutting themselves off from all visceral knowledge of God. It may be possible to experience the presence of God on your own, but like it or not, there is a depth, a rootedness, that is available only *within our tradition.* We experience this depth on the level of our viscera; all the words in the world cannot quite capture it for us.

There is also the *intuitive* level of grasping Communion, which is what I believe is intended by the expression "a personal relationship with Jesus Christ." Jesus is a person to us on an intuitive level, just as each of us is a whole person to him. We know each other personally and intuitively, and knowing each other and Jesus is what Communion is about. One of the dangers of focusing too much on the elements of Communion is to imagine that Jesus was more concerned with the bread than he was with the disciples. Exactly the opposite is true.

Imagine for a minute that, as Jesus was distributing the bread that evening in the upper room, and *after* he uttered the words, "this is my body," a stranger appeared at the door. According to Jewish custom, the stranger must be welcomed, and the Passover meal must be shared. So the stranger would be offered the bread. Would he be receiving the body of Christ? No, he would be receiving the Passover matzoh, the "bread of affliction which our fathers ate in the land of Egypt." The bread had become the body of Christ *only for the disciples.* "This is my body, which is given *for you*" (emphasis mine).

This truth has nothing to do with courtesy or exclusion. It has to do with faith. It is only when we accept Jesus *personally*—as one person accepting another person—that Communion becomes real for us. But accepting each other is something we do intuitively, naturally, subconsciously from the heart. The conscious, cognitive mind can be aware—sometimes—of some dimensions of the state of accepting a person. But our poor cognitive faculties are quickly overloaded, given the complexities of a human being, if we try to *think* our way into accepting someone. We have to turn that function over to our intuition, and our intuition can only accept a person *personally*—it doesn't operate on the level of theories.

When the administering priest utters the words, "This is my body which is for you," God is not setting forth a general principle nor proposing some theoretical statement, but rather making an intensely personal statement. "I am here, now, and I am making a claim on you. Jesus was born, and died, for *you*. His body is now offered, personally, to *you*. I love *you*. If you accept this, drink the juice and eat the bread." The Lord's Supper is the true confession of our acceptance of that love. It is at least the beginning of a personal relationship with Jesus Christ.

Now, anyone can read the words of the preceding paragraph; but only an *intuitive* knowledge of Communion can make them come alive. All the reading and talking about the Lord's Supper will not do it. That's why there's a sacrament in the first place.

The Mystery of Communion

In spite of the impressive gains of science, we human beings understand only a tiny fraction of creation. We can grasp algebra and Newtonian physics, perhaps even quantum mechanics or chaos theory. But the Lord's Supper is far more difficult to grasp than any of these. In fact, the mystery of Communion is ultimately too deep for *all* human knowledge. How, actually, the church and the world are changed by Communion is lost in the mists of unknowing that surround us.

A philosopher might argue that in our age, *science* is our myth (admittedly a very useful and powerful one), our way of convincing ourselves that we understand the world in which we live. But we really don't understand; we really aren't all that much smarter than the generations that have preceded us. Whether we are religious or not, we live in the midst of a mystery. Our human minds just don't "get" reality. Apparently they haven't been designed for that purpose. This is the lesson of the Tower of Babel. We cannot build a tower to God, either physical or mental. We must acknowledge our creatureliness, our limitations. There are great adventures of knowledge awaiting us, but when we arrive, we'll still be a long way from grasping God. We may climb the highest mountain, but we still can't touch the moon.

Our current myth—science—can't explain God at all. We

actually do better to approach God through the Lord's Supper than through science. Not that the sacrament can fully explain God to limited creatures such as we are, but it does open up the Mystery to us through other ways of knowing, ways that are unavailable to science.

Duties

Communion, like the other elements of worship, is first experienced as a series of duties. The sacrament is built around a number of commands from the Lord ("Take," "Eat," "Drink from it, all of you," "Do this in remembrance of me"). Every command entails a duty, and no dimension of worship has more commands than Communion—all this in spite of the fact that Communion, above all acts of worship, seems most intended for our benefit. Prayer, music, offering—these duties could be understood to be more for God's benefit than for that of the priests who are worshiping God. But not even scripture and sermon seem more exclusively for the benefit of the priests than the Lord's Supper. One may say that Communion is a means of grace through which God confers the blessing of the divine presence on those who serve. So it is critically important to recognize that the blessing of this element of worship—like the blessings of all elements of worship—is conferred through the performance of our duties.

The First Communion Duty: Preparation

As with any encounter in which some happy outcome is hoped for—applying for a job, submitting a book to a publisher, asking someone out on a date—so also is the spiritual encounter of Communion enriched and elevated by thorough and proper preparation. There is no mechanical quality about Communion, no rigid natural law that guarantees Communion will be meaningful, or that Christ's presence will be felt by the worshipers. "The wind blows where it chooses, and you hear the sound of it, but you do not know where it comes from or where it goes" (John 3:8). But surely, proper preparation is wise. How can a Christian spend more time preparing to go to the grocery store than he or she spends preparing to receive the body and blood of the Son of God?

For purely practical considerations, the amount of preparation will be related to the frequency with which your congregation celebrates the Lord's Supper. Elaborate preparations for the sacrament in a congregation where weekly observance is customary would perhaps put too great a strain on priests' time. On the other hand, if your congregation has Communion only four times a year, a week's preparation might be in order.

Some steps may be taken to prepare even before you arrive at church. For example, you may choose to:

1. Read a related scripture (Isa. 55; Mark 14:1–25; 1 Cor. 11:17–34) when you get up the morning of Communion.
2. Read a Communion devotion. (Ask your pastor for denominational resources.)
3. Fast, so that the body and blood of Christ is your first food of the day.

After the worship service has begun and the administering priest has made the invitation to the Table, you may offer an invitation of your own. Through prayer, invite those loved ones who have preceded you in death to sit with you for Communion.

Proper preparation will involve steps to rope off the Lord's Supper. Usually, these steps are corporate in nature and are determined by your tradition. Whatever they may be, I encourage you strongly to study and employ them. For example, when the time for Communion arrives, if there are people in the pews who simply do not believe that Jesus is from God (not doubters, now, but unbelievers—guests of other, or no, faith; the mildly curious), they should be given the opportunity to leave the sanctuary before the sacrament begins.

The Second Communion Duty: Maintaining Silence

When Elijah went to the door of the cave at Horeb, he heard the "still small voice" of God (1 Kings 19:11–13 RSV). The NRSV translates it as "a sound of sheer silence." If we are to hear God's voice in Communion, we too must listen acutely and in silence. Even something as simple as unwrapping a cough drop can mask the voice of God. The human mind is easily distracted from God by noise, especially speech. So avoid unnecessary speech, and be patient as Communion concludes. Remember that your voice will distract not only the person to whom you speak, but also a number of people with whom you are not even trying to communicate.

The Third Communion Duty: Service

Here I betray my prejudice for Communion in the pews. You have a sacred duty, as a priest of God, to offer the body and blood of Christ to at least one other believer. As you take the tray from the leader, or person sitting next to you, you allow that person to fulfill *his or her* priestly responsibility. Likewise, as you turn and offer the tray to the next person, you serve as a priest to that believer. You too handle the body and blood, not just for yourself, but for the person next to you, and through them, for the entire congregation.

Let me hold your attention to this truth: You are a priest not simply for yourself, but for the whole body, the whole congregation into which you are grafted. This is the meaning of your receiving and passing the trays. Through this most priestly act, you physically express the interconnection you have spiritually with God, with your neighbor, and with the whole church. It is this interconnection of the entire body that, Paul warns us, must be discerned during the Lord's Supper.

I would also recommend that your service to your neighbor include the words "the body of Christ" when you offer the bread, and "the blood of Christ" when you offer the wine. Such confessions help raise awareness (your own, as well as your neighbor's) of the holiness of what you are handling and offering, as well as your own willingness to fulfill your priestly duty.

A colleague and dear friend of mine prefers that the members of the congregation come forward to receive Communion. His reasoning is that those receiving Communion appreciate the sacred quality of the sacrament more when they actually have to stand up and move forward to receive the elements. This view accords with what I have said above regarding the sensory knowledge of Communion (specifically, its kinesthetic dimension). The danger is that the priests in the pew misinterpret the action of moving forward to receive Communion as necessitated by some shortcoming in their priesthood (that is, the impression that only the minister is authorized by God to offer the body and blood of Christ). This misinterpretation may perhaps be offset by choosing a priest from the pew to administer the sacrament to those who have themselves served the congregation—visibly, with forethought, precision, and deliberate action—after (or even before) the rest of the congregation has been served.

The Fourth Communion Duty: Remembrance

Fulfill the command to "do this in remembrance of me." As you feed on the body and blood, remember Christ as an infant; remember him as a 12-year-old in the Temple; remember him as an adult reading scripture in the synagogue, healing the leper, teaching the crowds from a boat on the sea; remember him picking up children, cleansing the Temple, breaking bread with his disciples. Remember him walking through grain fields, celebrating at a wedding, standing before Pilate. Remember him carrying the cross to Golgotha, being taken down and laid in a tomb, appearing to his disciples by the Sea of Galilee, risen from the grave.

The Fifth Communion Duty: Discerning the Body

As the service concludes, notice what has happened to the body that you are commanded to discern. It has been nourished on the body and blood of Jesus. It is fed, it is filled, it is pulled together, it is transformed. Grace has been poured upon the wounds of the church.

Furthermore, because we have been fed on the one loaf, we remain one body as we move out the doors and into the parking lot, and from there to our homes and the world. Christ is once more em*bodied* in the world; the incarnation lives again in the darkness, and the darkness cannot overcome it. If the administering priest does not say so on behalf of the gathered people, you as an individual priest should confess with thanks that the body has gathered for spiritual food, has been fed, and now moves out into the world as the incarnation of Christ.

REVIEW QUESTIONS

1. List the five duties of Communion described above.
2. What three correctives are proposed to our cognitive knowledge of Communion?
3. What is the "body" Paul speaks of in 1 Corinthians 11:29?
4. List the three principal sources of action in the Lord's Supper.
5. How were the disciples prepared—on that day and in their lives—for the Lord's Supper?
6. What means of preparation for Communion are mentioned in this chapter?
7. How does unadorned Communion degenerate into casual Communion?

DISCUSSION QUESTIONS

1. How would you describe your own experience of Communion?
2. How does your tradition rope off the Lord's Supper?
3. Share a story about Jesus that you will recall the next time the congregation celebrates the Lord's Supper.
4. Which means of preparation listed above have you employed? Which would you like to try? Can you think of others?
5. Compose a confession of thanks that "discerns the body" for use at the conclusion of the next Communion.

Chapter 8

Natural Worship

All the earth worships you.

—Psalm 66:4

Worship was once an integral part of the human experience. We evolved worshiping. Worship is more deeply ingrained in us than virtually any of the habits demanded of us by this very recent condition we call technology. Whether it would be advantageous, or even possible, to outgrow our drive to worship at some point in the future, for the present it would be foolish to imagine that we can suppress or deny this basic dimension of our existence without serious repercussions. Intuitively, there seems a connection between the lack of true worship in our society and the bizarre behaviors that seem to be happening with greater frequency as these years go by: mothers murdering their children, people shooting each other over violations of driving etiquette, acts of terrorism against our own people. This book is not the place to unravel that connection, but I have confidence that recovering our awareness of God's presence in our lives will soothe the fever that is producing our cultural hallucinations.

Understanding the critical role of worship in our lives has two ramifications. First, it is not a *culturally imposed* need, like deodorant or fast cars. It is a need ingrained in us by God's providential hand. All of creation is designed to reflect God's glory—the stars with their massive displays of light and heat; the eagle with its soaring grandeur; the valleys resplendent with wildflowers; and human beings, in our worship. When we worship, we simply fulfill our true role in creation; we display our connection to everything that is; we take our place. For all our many achievements, there's nothing like worship that says to the depths of our souls that we belong. Nor does any other activity do so much to shape our continuing growth in line with the will of our Creator.

And second, since worship is ingrained in us, it will not require rocket science to lead us to right worship. The path to God is in our genes and our routines. The routines (rituals) of worship not only express the love for God of which we are already aware; they also *grow* that love by cultivating in us worship as a mode of being. If we will simply train ourselves to experience worship as a mode of being, *as* we perform the routines of worship and *by* performing the routines of worship, we will find God all around us. We will find ourselves at home in the One in whom we live, move, and have our being.

Life, after all, is not merely thought. We can analyze problems of life, but we can't grasp life itself in its incredible complexity with our limited conscious minds. Successful life requires the intuition of a maturing soul, and the soul grows best in the soil of true worship.

Worship is the routine work we do for God—personally, directly, communally. All of the duties outlined in this book are important in themselves, but the cumulative effect is more important still. When we pay attention to our worship duties, we begin to find the path to what the ancients called piety and to worship as a mode of being that opens us to the religious presence of mind and to the experience of God. It is my conviction that we stumble blindly and discontentedly through a spiritual wasteland until we recognize and fulfill the simple duties we have as children of God.

It isn't too much to say that worship, true worship, is the very foundation and wellspring of life. Out of worship comes the joy of meaning and purpose, the strength to bear the heavy loads, the inspiration to do and say the right thing, the vision to make the big decisions, and the willingness to express the love through which, ultimately, we have our greatest effect on the world.

Spiritual Hygiene

My concern is that you may have tried to absorb the instructions of this book, and now feel overwhelmed at the sheer number of duties associated with worship. Worship may suddenly have taken on the appearance of an overwhelming task, when you have always looked upon it as a source of strength and uplift.

It may help to bear in mind that God *designs* us for worship—to do the work and to reap the benefits. Worship is work the way personal hygiene is work—it takes a while to develop good habits, but the benefits are felt immediately and continue to grow with each passing year. You learned to brush your teeth and wash behind your ears; you can learn to pray a prayer of preparation and discuss the sermon. Worship is spiritual hygiene. Just like personal hygiene, it's something everyone has to do; it's a routine everyone has to develop. If God had not given you teeth, you wouldn't need a toothbrush; if God had not given you ears, you wouldn't need to wash behind them. If God had not given you a soul, you wouldn't need worship.

You may say, if God loves us, why should we have to do all this work for God when we worship? If God's grace is sufficient for me, doesn't all this duty stuff sound a lot like salvation through works?

Well, if God were really keeping track, I don't think one hour a week of prayer, singing, and listening would likely be enough to offset the other 167 hours a week we spend in other pursuits. In fact, the work of worship is so remarkably easy once it has become habit that, on the day of judgment, it would hardly seem prudent to claim righteousness based upon the work done in worship.

Jesus says, "Take my yoke upon you . . . my yoke is easy, and my burden is light" (Matt. 11:29, 30). Yes, there is a yoke of worship, but its burden is light. We are not working to obtain God's blessing, any more than we exercise to obtain a pair of lungs and a heart. If I have been smoking heavily and watching TV all day while I eat boxes of chocolates and jelly doughnuts, shall I complain to God for having to develop new habits to get in shape and stay there? My soul is no different. Like my body, my soul is a blessing from God, which I must exercise to keep in shape.

The hardest thing about the transition is not the *duties* of worship—any particular one of them or all of them taken together. The hardest shift is in our unspoken *attitude* toward worship. The core of worship was once understood, unconsciously, to be service for God. It was for God's sake that we worshiped, not our own. But the last fifty years or so have seen the "death" of God ("disappearance" would be a better term, as the sense of worship as a mode of being has evaporated from so many of our churches) and the rise of consumerism, which teaches us—again, unconsciously—to expect benefit from worship *as worship's first and only reason for being.* It is supposed to make us better people or comfort us; to challenge us or stabilize our lives. Lately there's been a drive to link worship with lower stress and healthier bodies. Well, all of this may be true. I would argue that all of it *is* true. But *none* of it is the first purpose of worship. The first purpose of worship is to commit direct acts of love for God. Once we accept this fact and put it into practice, we begin to worship.

One of the negative effects of consumerism is self-absorption. Has there ever been a culture on the face of the earth more self-absorbed than we are? We are so self-absorbed that we don't even realize we're self-absorbed. We evaluate worship based on how it affects us! Jesus, who loves us profoundly, in giving us the commandment that is first of all, utters a gentle but prophetic word to all of us: "Worship isn't about *you.* It's about *God.* Worship isn't about what you get out of it. It's about what you put into it."

Your Priesthood

Because the Protestant tradition automatically heard "Catholic" when it heard the word "priest," we very early turned our backs on the term. In so doing, we not only surrendered a biblical truth *and* a central doctrine of our own tradition, but we hid ourselves from reality.

Every organization has a certain structure, and people within the structure are given titles and positions that make structure possible and, at the same time, draw boundaries between people. For example, you may be a U.S. citizen, but perhaps not a government official. Or you may be a government official, but perhaps not an *elected* official. Or you may be an elected official, but not the president. There is clearly a structure, a hierarchy, to our government. This is true of all governments, all businesses, even all churches.

The presence of structure in the church, however, does not mean that there are *professional* worshipers—pastors, music directors, liturgists, (who might be called "priests" in another tradition)—and then, separated by a religious boundary, *ordinary* worshipers (the people in the pews, the "laity"). The reality is that *everyone who worships God is a priest.* Reality looks like this:

1. The work of worship is left to the priest. You do the work of worship. Therefore, you are a priest.
2. The rituals of worship are performed by a priest. You perform the rituals of worship. Therefore, you are a priest.
3. The priest is the one who presents offerings to God. You "present your bod[y] as a living sacrifice, holy and acceptable to God" (Rom. 12:1). Therefore, you are a priest.
4. God speaks to the priest in worship. God speaks to you. Therefore, you are a priest.
5. The closeness to God, which is called here the religious presence of mind, is a special gift of the priesthood. You experience the religious presence of mind. Therefore, you belong to the priesthood.

We have outgrown the stage in human development when we can count on others to experience God for us. Such a vicarious relationship with God no longer seems authentic. An indirect relationship simply does not satisfy our spiritual hunger. But the only direct relationship with God belongs to the priest, so let us be thankful that we are the priesthood. Let us apply ourselves to the training that is our inheritance, and "worship the LORD with gladness" (Ps. 100:2).

"Attending" Church

The first critical duty of every Christian (every priest) is regular attendance at church. Absence from church is not only a violation of the fourth commandment ("Remember the sabbath day, and keep it holy." Ex. 20:8), but it is a violation of the commandment that Jesus calls "first of all," namely, "You shall love the Lord your God with all your heart, and with all your soul, and with all your mind, and with all your strength . . . You shall love your neighbor as yourself" (Mark 12:30–31).

When we become too self-absorbed, we lose sight of how being in church is an act of love toward our neighbors. Let me give you just one dimension to illustrate. All of us have weeks in which it seems difficult, if not impossible, to see the world as Jesus says it really is. A loved one has died; a noble attempt has failed; the stress at home or at work has been nearly unbearable. The last time you attended church, *someone* sitting near you was having one of those difficult weeks. I guarantee it. When that person saw you, his or her spirits were lifted, if ever so slightly, because of the realization of being in the midst of "a royal priesthood, a holy nation" (1 Peter 2:9). You ministered to that person just by showing up, without your even being aware of it. Your ministry of presence produces fruit by simply being there in worship as a priest. And as much as your presence is felt, so is your absence. There is no way to escape your influence on the congregation. There is no way to avoid the commandment to love your neighbor as yourself as far as worship is concerned.

Even more obvious is the connection between church attendance and the other half of the commandment (that is, to love God). The priesthood of all believers means that *every true Christian is a priest.* I have heard it said, "I'm a Christian, but I don't go to church." What is meant by the word *Christian* in that statement? Apparently, it has something to do with trying to be good, and perhaps is related to the church-going habits of parents or grandparents. But the contradiction in the statement quickly comes to life if we substitute an equivalent expression for the word *Christian.* Since every Christian is a priest, the statement "I'm a *Christian,* but I don't go to church" is equivalent to the statement, "I'm a *priest,* but I don't go to church."

How can you be a priest and not go to church? It's like being a surgeon and never going to the hospital, or a fireman and never going to the fire station. If a person is entitled to make claims for himself or herself without actually performing the functions that those claims entail, you can be the quarterback for the Miami Dolphins, and I'll be an All-pro wide receiver!

Seriously, the mark of a Christian is absolute surrender to the absolute Good. It means accepting as eternally true and valid Jesus' claim that the commandment which is first of all is the commandment to love God. To love someone—anyone—is to love that person on his or her own terms. To love God on *God's* terms is to worship.

The Church's Imperfections

I will grant you that many times in the past, the human institution of the church has understood the expression "absolute surrender to God" as "absolute surrender to the religious authorities." As human beings, we easily confuse our own authority with the power of God, our own plans with the will of God, our own opinions with the wisdom of God. (The church, of course, has no monopoly on this behavior—it is found in politics, business, art—every human endeavor.) Traditions, customs, and rituals are not automatically right for our time just because they were right for some earlier time. God continues to breathe change into human history.

But as Presbyterians, who are "Reformed and always reforming," we neither accept the traditions of human beings as the ultimate will of God, nor reject *all* tradition because it is the tradition of human beings. (After all, we are human beings ourselves.) Somewhere in our worship—in the music, the prayers, the scripture, the sermon, and the offering—somewhere in all that, we are expressing our love for God, and we are experiencing God's love for us. And somehow we know this has taken place when we leave the sanctuary.

Again, I will grant that many a particular worship service leaves us without a sense that we have spent the past hour loving God and each other. Part of this is probably due to insufficient preparation on the part of each priest in the congregation, and part may be due to insufficient preparation (and/or training) on the part of those charged with leading worship.

Neither of these reasons, though, is grounds for abandoning our priestly function. Does a teacher stop coming to class because the students aren't getting their homework done? Do you just park your car and walk away from it because it isn't running right? As priests of God, we have the obligation, in fact the need (one of the few true needs of human beings) to correct the situation. Any other response diminishes our humanity.

Using This Book

I'm guessing that you did not develop the habit of brushing your teeth from hearing one toothpaste commercial. It may be that your mother had to remind you once or twice in your formative years. Similarly, I would not expect someone to read this book once and suddenly become a perfected priest, constantly aware of worship as a mode of being, and continually experiencing the religious presence of mind. So I invite you to spend time with the idea of your priesthood and with the duties outlined above. The real fruit of your study will take months to mature.

For instance, you might want to start working with this book on some date that is important to you, for example, your birthday, the anniversary of your baptism, Pentecost, or the birthday of your local congregation. On the first day of your study, start a journal about your experience of worship up to that point in your life, your spiritual journey, your relationships with your partners in faith. Then, for the next several months, read the chapter on prayer every Sunday morning before worship. Make an effort to fulfill your prayer duties every Sunday for two months, until they become ingrained habits.

Then spend two months in the same way reading about your music duty; two months on scripture and sermon, and so forth. Read the chapter on Communion before *every* Communion service (at least a week before, and then on the morning of Communion). If your tradition celebrates Communion every Sunday, reading the chapter on Communion can be handled the same way as the others—two months straight. If your church celebrates the Lord's Supper less frequently, you will need to plan ahead to remember your discipline and adjust your schedule with the other chapters accordingly.

Spend the year between the day you begin and the first anniversary of that date converting these worship duties into habits. (You should find yourself with a two-month cushion to cover missed Sundays, and/or to work longer on those duties requiring more practice.) On the one-year anniversary of beginning this pilgrimage, take out your journal and write about the same topics you did when you began. Then compare your two journal entries.

Many folks find it easier to complete a course of study in the company of a spiritual partner who is also involved. Ideally, there will be a whole group in your church, and within that group, each person will have a worship partner.

A second good reason for studying with a group of church members is the effect on the whole worship service when *the majority of your congregation* understands and practices worship as work for God. Your whole *church* may well experience a rebirth. For this reason, I heartily encourage you to study this book with a group within your church. If your church already has a small group program, there may be a way to use this book as a curriculum. Or maybe an adult or youth Sunday school class could work on it together. If you can't pull a group together to journey with you, ask a friend. You may be surprised, though, to learn how many folks in your church are willing to try discipline as a way to think of worship, to act in worship, and to serve God.

Conclusion

I've felt excitement while writing this book for several reasons. As I have outlined the duties, I've recalled moments of worship (personal and corporate) when I was aware of God's presence, when I was blessed with a religious presence of mind. I have also become aware of the larger picture—the *cumulative* effect of worship on my life, touching nearly all dimensions and creating in me a deep sense of thanksgiving. But I also experience joy and excitement as I entertain the hope that you, the reader, may find the deep springs of the spirit, a regular visitation of the religious presence of mind, through your own developing discipline. I have come to appreciate in a very small way what Jesus meant when he told the disciples, "I have said these things to you so that my joy may be in you, and that your joy may be complete" (John 15:11).

Throughout this book, I have not attempted to in any way replace the Directory for Worship in our *Book of Order,* which in its normative dimension, at any rate, is devoted to worship as ritual. Nor, I hope, have I left the impression that I am attempting to force any particular practice on my fellow Presbyterians (an effort doomed to failure, as every Presbyterian already knows!). My goal has been a simple one: to foster an understanding of worship as work (acts of love) for God, and to encourage us all to take the specific steps necessary *to express this truth in our lives each time we worship,* in harmony with whatever theological reflections we may have on the subject. As fulfillment of the commandment which is first of all, worship is *the* fundamental action of life. In the Presbyterian tradition, we bring thought to bear on our actions, but *we still do the actions.* We still perform our duties. We still worship.

I recognize that the duties I have outlined here are only my best intuition of what honors and serves God. So let me join Martin Luther (lofty company for me!) in saying, "Indeed we beg through Christ, from the heart, if something better shall be revealed to those who are in advance of us in these things, that they command us to be silent so that by common work we may aid the common cause."[1]

REVIEW QUESTIONS

1. How is worship "spiritual hygiene"?
2. According to consumerism, what is the purpose of worship? What is its purpose according to faith?
3. List five realities that indicate your priesthood.
4. What is odd about the statement, "I'm a Christian, but I don't go to church"?
5. How does a believer love God on God's terms?
6. Describe the outline given for studying this book.
7. Give two reasons for studying this material with other church members.

DISCUSSION QUESTIONS

1. How would you assess your congregation's understanding of worship?
2. Which duties of worship seem easiest to you? Which seem hardest?
3. Do you have a spiritual partner with whom you can study this material?
4. How has your understanding of worship changed?
5. What further questions about worship remain for you?

Notes

Chapter 1. Three Dimensions of Worship

1. Evelyn Underhill, *Worship* (New York: Harper, 1936), 186.
2. Augustine, *Letters* 44.1.1, quoted in John Calvin, *Institutes of the Christian Religion,* ed. John T. McNeill, trans. Ford Lewis Battles (Philadelphia: Westminster Press, 1960), IV.10.14, pp. 1191–92.

Chapter 2. The Priesthood of All Believers

1. Ernst Troeltsch, *Protestantism and Progress* (New York, 1912) 159, quoted by E. Harris Harbison in *The Age of Reformation* (Ithaca, N.Y.: Cornell University Press, 1955).
2. Harbison, *The Age of Reformation,* 54.
3. "To the Christian Nobility of the German Nation concerning the Reform of the Christian Estate" (1520), in *A Reformation Reader: Primary Texts with Introductions,* ed. Denis R. Janz (Minneapolis, Minn.: Fortress, 1999), 91.
4. John Calvin, *Institutes,* IV.19.28, p. 1476.
5. *Dictionary of Baptists in America,* ed. Bill J. Leonard (Downers Grove, Ill.: InterVarsity Press, 1994), 225.
6. Walter B. Shurden, ed., *The Doctrine of the Priesthood of Believers* (Nashville: Convention Press, 1987), 9.
7. From John Davenport's "Creed," in *American Christianity,* H. Shelton Smith, Robert T. Handy, and Lefferts A. Loetscher (New York: Charles Scribner's Sons, 1960), 108. Davenport (1597–1669) was a Congregational minister in New Haven, Connecticut. His creed was held to be "a representative summary of 'The New England Way.'"

Chapter 3. The Duties of the Priest: Prayer

1. Quoted in Harry Emerson Fosdick, *The Meaning of Prayer* (Nashville: Abingdon Press, 1962), 3.

Chapter 4. The Duties of the Priest: Music

1. Basil of Caesarea, *Hom. in Ps. 1, PG* 29.211, quoted in "Music and Musician in Service to the Church," by Kathryn Nichols, *Reformed Liturgy and Music,* vol. 20, no. 2 (spring 1986): 75.
2. Ibid., Basil, *Hom. in Ps. 1; PG* 29.211.
3. Ibid., John Chrysostom, Hom. 5, *PG* 63.486–87.

Chapter 5. The Duties of the Priest: Scripture and Sermon

1. Bard Thompson, *Liturgies of the Western Church* (New York: Collins, 1962), 318.
2. *Reformed Liturgy and Music,* vol. 26, no. 3 (summer 1992), 121.

Chapter 6. The Duties of the Priest: The Offering

1. Heidelberg Catechism, Q. 1.

Chapter 7. The Duties of the Priest: Communion

1. *A Common Calling: The Witness of Our Reformation Churches in North America Today,* ed. Keith Nickle and Timothy F. Lull (Minneapolis: Augsburg, 1993), 41.
2. See, for example, Calvin, *Institutes,* IV.17.18, pp. 1380–81.

Chapter 8. Natural Worship

1. "Formula of Mass and Communion for the Church at Wittenberg, 1523"; quoted by Bard Thompson, *Liturgies of the Western Church,* 107.